ECDL® 5.0

European Computer Driving Licence

Module 3 - Word Processing

using Word 2003

Release ECDL243v1

Published by:

> CiA Training Ltd
> Business & Innovation Centre
> Sunderland Enterprise Park
> Sunderland SR5 2TA
> United Kingdom

> Tel: +44 (0) 191 549 5002
> Fax: +44 (0) 191 549 9005

> E-mail: info@ciatraining.co.uk
> Web: www.ciatraining.co.uk

> **ISBN-13: 978 1 86005 669 7**

The following information applies <u>only</u> to candidates in Ireland.

Acknowledgements:

> The European Computer Driving Licence is operated in Ireland by ICS Skills, the training and certification body of the Irish Computer Society.
> Candidates using this courseware should register online with ICS Skills through an approved ECDL Test Centre. Without a valid registration, and the allocation of a unique ICS Skills ID number or SkillsCard, no ECDL tests can be taken and no certificate, or any other form of recognition, can be given to a candidate.

> Other ECDL Foundation Certification programmes offered by ICS Skills include Equalskills, ECDL Advanced, ECDL WebStarter, ECDL ImageMaker, EUCIP and Certified Training Professional.

> Contact: ICS Skills
>   Crescent Hall
>   Mount Street Crescent
>   Dublin 2
>   Ireland

> Website: www.ics.ie/skills
> *Email:*   *skills@ics.ie*

First published 2008

European Computer Driving Licence, ECDL, International Computer Driving Licence, ICDL, e-Citizen and related logos are all registered Trade Marks of The European Computer Driving Licence Foundation Limited ("ECDL Foundation").

CiA Training Ltd is an entity independent of ECDL Foundation and is not associated with ECDL Foundation in any manner. This courseware may be used to assist candidates to prepare for the ECDL Foundation Certification Programme as titled on the courseware. Neither ECDL Foundation nor **CiA Training Ltd** warrants that the use of this courseware publication will ensure passing of the tests for that ECDL Foundation Certification Programme. This courseware publication has been independently reviewed and approved by ECDL Foundation as covering the learning objectives for the ECDL Foundation Certification Programme.

Confirmation of this approval can be obtained by reviewing the Partners Page in the About Us Section of the website www.ecdl.org

The material contained in this courseware publication has not been reviewed for technical accuracy and does not guarantee that candidates will pass the test for the ECDL Foundation Certification Programme. Any and all assessment items and/or performance-based exercises contained in this courseware relate solely to this publication and do not constitute or imply certification by ECDL Foundation in respect of the ECDL Foundation Certification Programme or any other ECDL Foundation test. Irrespective of how the material contained in this courseware is deployed, for example in a learning management system (LMS) or a customised interface, nothing should suggest to the candidate that this material constitutes certification or can lead to certification through any other process than official ECDL Foundation certification testing.

For details on sitting a test for an ECDL Foundation certification programme, please contact your country's designated National Licensee or visit the ECDL Foundation's website at www.ecdl.org.

Candidates using this courseware must be registered with the National Operator before undertaking a test for an ECDL Foundation Certification Programme. Without a valid registration, the test(s) cannot be undertaken and no certificate, nor any other form of recognition, can be given to a candidate. Registration should be undertaken with your country's designated National Licensee at an Approved Test Centre.

Downloading the Data Files

The data associated with these exercises must be downloaded from our website. Go to: *www.ciatraining.co.uk/data*. Follow the on screen instructions to download the appropriate data files.

By default, the data files will be downloaded to **My Documents \ CIA DATA FILES \ ECDL \ 3 Word Processing**.

If you prefer, the data can be supplied on CD at an additional cost. Contact the Sales team at *info@ciatraining.co.uk*.

Aims

To demonstrate the ability to use a word processing application on a personal computer to produce everyday letters and documents.

To understand and accomplish basic operations associated with creating, formatting and finishing a word processed document ready for its distribution.

To demonstrate some of the more advanced features covering creating standard tables, using pictures and images within a document, importing objects and using mail merge tools.

Objectives

After completing the guide the user will be able to:

- Work with documents and save them in different file formats
- Choose built in options to enhance productivity
- Create and edit small word processing documents that will be ready to share and distribute
- Apply different formats to documents to enhance them before distribution; recognise good practice in choosing the appropriate formatting options
- Insert tables, images and drawn objects into documents
- Prepare documents for mail merge operations
- Adjust document page settings and check and correct spelling before finally printing documents.

Assessment of Knowledge

At the end of this guide is a section called the **Record of Achievement Matrix**. Before the guide is started it is recommended that the user completes the matrix to measure the level of current knowledge.

Tick boxes are provided for each feature. **1** is for no knowledge, **2** some knowledge and **3** is for competent.

After working through a section, complete the matrix for that section and only when competent in all areas move on to the next section.

Contents

Section 1
Getting Started

By the end of this Section you should be able to:

Start *Word*

Recognise the Screen Layout

Use the Menus and Toolbars

Use Help and the Office Assistant

Exit *Word*

To gain an understanding of the above features, work through the **Driving Lessons** in this **Section**.

For each **Driving Lesson**, read the **Park and Read** instructions, without touching the keyboard, then work through the numbered steps of the **Manoeuvres** on the computer. Complete the **Revision Exercise(s)** at the end of the section to test your knowledge.

Driving Lesson 1 - Starting Word

🅟 Park and Read

Word is an extremely useful word processing application with lots of features. The following exercises introduce you to the application, to help get you started. There are numerous ways to start the program. The following method is recommended for beginners.

☞ Manoeuvres

1. Click once on **start** to show the **Start** menu. All *Windows* applications can be started here. Move the mouse pointer over **All Programs** and then click on 🖼 Microsoft Office Word 2003.

ℹ️ *Depending on individual installations, Word may be located within a **Microsoft Office 2003** folder, as in the diagram.*

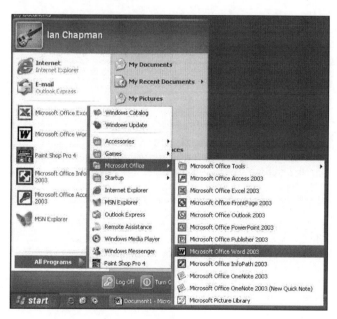

ℹ️ *If Word has been used recently there may be an entry for it in the **Start** menu and it can be started from there by clicking the entry.*

Driving Lesson 2 - Layout of the Word Screen

🅿 Park and Read

When *Word* starts, the user is presented with a screen with a menu at the top and a bar along the bottom.

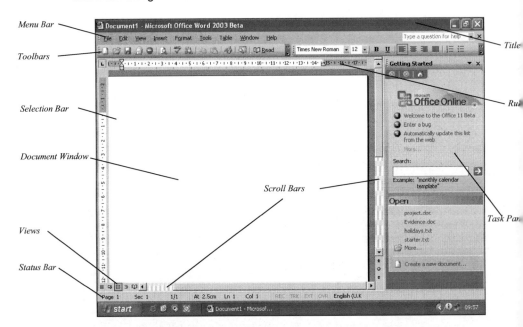

The top line is called the **Title Bar** and denotes the application and current document in use. Below there is a **Menu Bar** where commands are selected using the mouse. Below the Menu Bar is another bar, containing two **Toolbars**. These bars contain buttons that are used to access the most commonly used menu commands. Using the **Toolbars** greatly improves the speed of work.

At the right of the screen is an area called the **Task Pane**, which helps to perform some common tasks. It can be changed depending on the task currently being performed. Various types of **Task Pane** are available.

At the bottom of the screen is a bar called the **Status Bar**, where information is displayed relating to the task on which the user is currently working.

Driving Lesson 2 - Continued

Manoeuvres

1. When certain options are selected in *Word 2003* the program tries to download content from **Office Online**, by connecting to the Internet. This can become annoying, especially for users without an Internet connection, or with a slow, dial up connection. While working through this guide, disable the option. Select **Tools | Options**, make sure the **General** tab is selected and click **Service Options**. A new window will appear; select **Online Content** from the list on the left.

2. If the **Show content and links from Office Online** box is checked, uncheck it and click **OK**. If it is not checked, just click **OK**. Click **OK** again to close the **Options** dialog box. This change will not take effect until *Word* is restarted in a later Driving Lesson.

3. Use the diagram on the previous page to locate the various parts of the screen. If the **Task Pane** is not visible, select **View | Task Pane**.

4. If the **Office Assistant** is visible, right click on it and select **Hide** to remove it from the screen. This will be described in more detail later.

Driving Lesson 3 - Menu Bar

▣ Park and Read

The **Menu Bar** contains all of the commands needed to use *Word*, within drop down lists. When *Word* starts, the **Menu Bar** displays the full range of commands. However, as they are used, the most common commands selected move to the top of the list and the rest are hidden. The hidden commands can be revealed at any time. If a command is not used for some time, it will stop appearing on the short, personalised menu.

> ℹ️ *The menus may look different to those in this guide because of this customisation feature, but the principles remain the same.*

↱ Manoeuvres

1. Move the pointer over the word **Edit** and click with the left mouse button to open the **Edit** menu.

2. Notice how some of the commands are ghosted (pale coloured). This means they are not available for selection at the moment. Chevrons appear at the bottom of the list for a few seconds and will expand the menu if clicked on. If not, the full list will appear. Click on **Edit** again to close the menu.

3. To use the chevrons, click on **Edit** and immediately click the chevrons at the bottom of the drop down list to expand it.

4. Close the **Edit** menu by either clicking outside the menu or click on **Edit** again.

> ℹ️ *The menu can also be expanded by double clicking on it. If one menu is expanded, the others are expanded automatically.*

Driving Lesson 3 - Continued

5.   Double click the **Insert** menu to open it. Three dots after a command
      indicate that a further selection is available from a dialog box. Click
      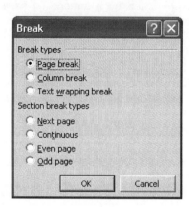 to display the **Break** dialog box.

6.   Read the options available then click **Cancel** to close the dialog box.

7.   Click **Insert** again. If necessary, expand the menu and find
      Bookmark... . This option may have a paler shade of colour to
      the left than some of the others. This indicates that it is not currently part
      of the personalised menu.

8.   Click on **Bookmark** to display the **Bookmark** dialog box. After reading the
      options, select **Cancel** to close the dialog box.

9.   Now click **Insert** again. Notice how **Bookmark** now appears in the short
      version of the menu. Click on **Insert** again to close the menu.

10.   An arrow after a command denotes that another menu will appear. Click
      View, then rest the mouse pointer over Toolbars ▶ .

11.   A further menu appears. Click on **View** again to close the menu.

12.   Continue experimenting by displaying the contents of the other menu
      options.

Driving Lesson 4 - Toolbars

🅿 Park and Read

Toolbars allow quick access to the most commonly used commands and each command is represented by a button. To save space on the screen, many buttons are hidden, but they can easily be displayed. The toolbars become personalised after being used, the frequently used buttons replacing others on the toolbar, which are then hidden.

ℹ️ *The toolbars may look different to those in this guide because of this customisation feature, but the principles remain the same.*

☞ Manoeuvres

1. The **Toolbars** are just beneath the **Menu Bar**, resting on the same line.

      Standard Toolbar   *Formatting Toolbar*

2. With no menus open, move the mouse pointer over a button on the **Toolbar** and leave it there for a few seconds.

3. A **ToolTip** appears, ![Save], showing the name of the button. Read the **ToolTips** for each of the visible buttons.

4. Chevrons, ![chevron], on a toolbar indicate that not all buttons on this toolbar can be seen. Click the chevrons at the right of the **Standard Toolbar**. Now a box appears showing all of the buttons from the **Standard Toolbar**.

5. Rest the mouse pointer over **Add or Remove Buttons | Standard** from the bottom of this box to see all of the buttons which could be placed on the **Standard** toolbar.

6. Those with ticks are either on the main toolbar, or the hidden toolbar. Click the tick next to the **Format Painter** button, ![Format Painter Ctrl+Shift+C], to remove it from the toolbar (if this button has already been removed, click to replace it, then repeat step **18** again to remove it).

7. To return toolbars to their state when *Word* was first opened for this session, click **Add or Remove Buttons | Standard**, move the pointer down to the bottom of the list of buttons and click **Reset Toolbar**.

Driving Lesson 4 - Continued

8. To see the complete **Standard** and the **Formatting** toolbars at the same time, click the chevrons at the right of the **Standard** toolbar and select **Show Buttons on Two Rows**.

9. Click the arrow at the right of either toolbar and select **Show Buttons on One Row** to replace them in the original orientation.

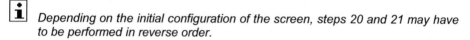

Depending on the initial configuration of the screen, steps 20 and 21 may have to be performed in reverse order.

10. Toolbars can also be moved manually. Move the mouse pointer over the dashed bar,  at the left of the **Formatting** toolbar, until it changes to a four headed arrow, as in the diagram below:

11. Click and hold down the mouse, then drag it towards the centre of the screen. Release the button and the toolbar should be 'floating', with its own **Title Bar**.

12. Using the title bar, drag the toolbar to the left until it is in line with the left side of the screen.

13. Move the **Formatting** toolbar back to the top, next to the **Standard** toolbar, positioning it so that each toolbar takes up about half of the row.

14. Select **View | Toolbars** to see the toolbars currently available. The toolbars currently in use have a tick next to them.

15. Any listed toolbar can be added to the screen by clicking on it. Click the **Picture** toolbar and it appears on the screen.

16. Move the **Picture** toolbar up to the right of the **Formatting** toolbar, by dragging its **Title Bar**.

17. To remove the **Picture** toolbar from the screen, select **View | Toolbars** and click on **Picture** again, or click the **Close** button, ☒, at the top right corner of the toolbar.

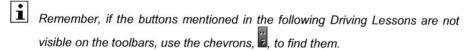

Remember, if the buttons mentioned in the following Driving Lessons are not visible on the toolbars, use the chevrons, ⋮ to find them.

Driving Lesson 5 - Task Pane

🅿 Park and Read

The **Task Pane** provides options for performing some common tasks. It appears, disappears and changes depending on the task currently being performed.

↱ Manoeuvres

1. The **Task Pane** at the right of the screen helps perform common tasks more quickly. To see the available panes click the drop down arrow at the right of **Getting Started Task Pane**.

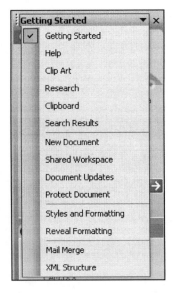

2. Click on **Styles and Formatting** to display this **Task Pane**.

3. In the same way, look at each of the available **Task Panes**.

4. To hide the **Task Pane**, either click its **Close** button or select **View | Task Pane**.

ℹ️ *Remember, if the buttons mentioned in the following Driving Lessons are not visible on the toolbars, use the chevrons,* ⟩⟩, *to find them.*

Driving Lesson 6 - Help

▣ Park and Read

Word has a comprehensive **Help** facility. This means that full advantage can be taken of the features incorporated in the program. Using **Help** can usually solve the majority of problems encountered.

⌕ Manoeuvres

1. Select **Help | Microsoft Office Word Help** to display the **Help** options in the **Task Pane**.

i *If the **Office Assistant** appears when this selection is made, hide it by clicking on the **Options** button on the yellow dialog box, then selecting the **Options** tab and clicking on the **Use the Office Assistant** check box to remove the check. Click **OK**, then repeat step **1**.*

2. **Help** can be searched for in two ways. Either type in keywords into the **Search for** box or search through the **Table of Contents**.

3. Type **Insert** into the **Search for** box and click →.

4. The search results appear in the **Task Pane**. Select **Insert a picture** from the list. Notice that this will show the help in a new window.

5. From the two results select **Insert a picture from a file**.

6. Read the help then close the window using the **Close** button, ⊠.

7. Click the **Back** button, ⊕, at the top of the **Task Pane**.

8. Select **Table of Contents**, ⊞ Table of Contents. Notice how the help topics are grouped into sections.

9. Select **Working with Text** from the list, all topics associated with working with text will appear below and slightly indented form the main sections.

10. Select **Select text and graphics**, a new window will appear.

11. Read the help then close the help window.

12. Close the **Task Pane**.

i *Help also contains a **Detect and Repair** feature, which repairs some registry and application settings. If problems are experienced running Word, select **Help | Detect and Repair**, then follow the on screen instructions.*

Driving Lesson 7 - The Office Assistant

▣ Park and Read

The **Office Assistant** provides instant on-screen help on tasks currently being undertaken. It is an animated character, which produces a light bulb when it knows a quicker way of doing the current task, or knows a handy tip. The **Office Assistant** can also help by answering questions. It remains on screen until it is removed.

☞ Manoeuvres

1. Select **Help | Show the Office Assistant** to display the **Office Assistant**, who appears with a **What would you like to do?** dialog box.

ℹ *If the dialog box doesn't appear, click once on the **Office Assistant**.*

2. In the white box, type **Toolbars** and click on **Search**. A list of help options appears in the **Task Pane**.

3. Move the mouse over **Show or hide a toolbar** until the cursor changes to 🖑, then click once to display the help in a new window.

4. Select **Show a Toolbar** from the list. Read the **Help**, then close the window and the **Task Pane**.

5. Click on the **Office Assistant** again and select **Options** from the dialog box. The **Office Assistant** dialog box appears.

ℹ *If the **Assistant** does not move out of the way and blocks the view of the screen, it can be moved by clicking and dragging.*

Driving Lesson 7 - Continued

6. Options can be changed to suit individual requirements. Select the **Gallery** tab, then click the **Next** button to see another character. Keep clicking **Next** to see the characters which can represent the **Assistant**.

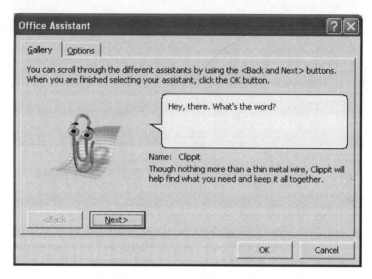

[i] *The **Assistant** can only be changed if the Office CD is in the CD-ROM drive.*

7. Click the **Options** tab. To stop the **Assistant** appearing automatically, click the **Use the Office Assistant** check box to remove the check.

8. Read through the other available options.

9. Click **Cancel** to close the dialog box without changing or removing the **Assistant**.

10. Click with the right mouse button on the **Assistant** and select **Animate!** to see one of the character's animations. Try it again to see a different animation.

11. Right click on the **Assistant** again and select **Hide** to remove it.

12. Close *Word*, using the **Close** button, [X], on the **Title Bar**.

Driving Lesson 8 - Revision

This covers the features introduced in this section. Try not to refer to the preceding Driving Lessons while completing it.

1. Start *Word*.

2. Select **Help | Microsoft Office Word Help** (if the **Office Assistant** is displayed, change the options to stop it appearing).

3. Using the **Search for** box, find and read the help about how **Create a chart** (use **chart** as the keyword).

4. Use the **Table of Contents** to locate help on **Page and Line Numbers** (within **Formatting Documents**), then select **Format page numbers** option and display the help.

5. Close **Help**.

6. Ask the **Office Assistant** the following question: **How do I print?**

7. Select **Print a document** from the list and read the help.

8. Close the **Help** window and the **Task Pane** and hide the **Assistant**.

9. List the **ToolTips** by placing the mouse pointer over the following buttons:

a)   b)   c)   d)   e)   f)   g)   h)

10. Search for **Copy** using the **Office Assistant**. Find out how to copy a table.

11. Use the **Office Assistant**, and **help** as your search word, how many **About getting help while you work** entries are identified?

12. Close the **Search Results** and hide the **Assistant**.

    Display the **Word Help Task Pane** and select the **Table of Contents**.

13. Open the **Formatting Documents** book then the **Margins and Page Set up** book.

14. Display the help about **Change page margins**.

15. Close **Help** and then close *Word*.

i   *Check the answers at the back of the guide.*

If you experienced any difficulty completing the Revision, refer back to the Driving Lessons in this section. Then redo the Revision.

Once you are confident with the features, complete the Record of Achievement Matrix referring to the section at the end of the guide. Only when competent move on to the next Section.

Section 2
Documents

By the end of this Section you should be able to:

Enter Text

Work in Different Views

Open, Save and Close Documents

Save a Document in Different Formats

Save Documents as Templates

Save Versions of Documents

To gain an understanding of the above features, work through the **Driving Lessons** in this **Section**.

For each **Driving Lesson**, read the **Park and Read** instructions, without touching the keyboard, then work through the numbered steps of the **Manoeuvres** on the computer. Complete the **Revision Exercise(s)** at the end of the section to test your knowledge.

Driving Lesson 9 - Entering Text

▣ Park and Read

It is not necessary to press the <**Enter**> key at the end of each line as the computer automatically detects the end of a line and starts a new one. This is called **Word Wrap**. <**Enter**> is only used to force a new line, i.e. to end a paragraph, to add a blank line or to start a new line at any time.

<**Shift**> is used to enter a capital letter (or <**Caps Lock**> if a large amount of text is to be capitalised). <**Tab**> is used to advance the insertion point to the next tab stop.

To move the insertion point around a document, either use the mouse and click or use the **Cursor Arrow Keys**.

⌐ Manoeuvres

1.   Start *Word*. A new, blank document is automatically opened.

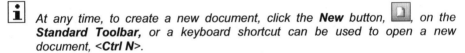 *At any time, to create a new document, click the* **New** *button,* , *on the* **Standard Toolbar,** *or a keyboard shortcut can be used to open a new document,* <**Ctrl N**>.

2.   Enter the following text (use <**Enter**> twice to separate the two paragraphs at this stage, although it is not the best way to space paragraphs. Paragraph spacing in covered later in Driving Lesson 60):

> A computer is an electronic machine that is automatically controlled; it can store a vast amount of information and works at fantastically high speeds. Computers do not have brains, the thinking is done by humans, who feed them information and program them to perform particular tasks.

> The first electronic computers were constructed in the 1940s using valves, which were large and gave off a lot of heat. The invention of transistors and later the integrated circuit (silicon chips), led to computers becoming smaller and smaller with greatly increased power.

 *This text is saved as* **Typing** *in the next Driving Lesson.*

ⓘ *Jagged red lines may have appeared under words that are misspelled. Do not do anything about these, as spell checking will be covered in a later section.*

Driving Lesson 10 - Saving Documents

▣ Park and Read

If text is to be used again it must be saved. There are two main ways to save a document: **Save As** and **Save**. **Save As** allows file name, file type and location to be specified and is therefore always used to save a newly created document, i.e. a document that has not been named. When a document has already been saved, i.e. been given a name, **File | Save** can be used to save/update the current changes in that document. If an existing document is to be used as the basis for a new one, but the original must not be overwritten, then it must be saved with a new name after the changes are made.

i *When a new document is to be saved, selecting **Save** displays the same dialog box as **Save As**.*

↻ Manoeuvres

1. Make sure that the data files for this module have been downloaded (see **Downloading the Data Files** on page 3). The data by default is stored in the folder **My Documents\CIA DATA FILES\ECDL\3 Word Processing**.

i *If a different folder is being used, make sure data is saved to the correct location.*

2. Select the **File** menu and choose the **Save As** command. The **Save As** dialog box appears.

3. Enter the name of the file in the **File name** box. In this instance, the file is to be called **Typing**.

Driving Lesson 10 - Continued

i *A filename can be of any length. Choose a meaningful name but do not use any of the following characters: ><"*?:\ /;|.*

4.   The **My Documents** folder is selected from the **Places Bar** by default. To save to the data files folder, with **My Documents** selected in the **Save in** box, double click on **CIA DATA FILES**, double click on **ECDL** and finally double click on **3 Word Processing**.

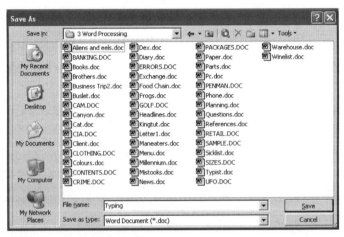

i *If the data is to be saved in another location, e.g. a floppy disk or memory stick, make sure **Save in** shows this location.*

5.   To see the different levels of folders in **My Documents**, click on the drop down arrow to the right of the **Save in** box. The hierarchy of folders should be shown, similar to the diagram to the right.

6.   Click **Save** to complete the save.

7.   At the bottom of the document, press <Enter> twice. Type in **This document was created by**, then enter your name.

8.   You need to keep the original document, so you will save the version with the text added in step 7 with another name. Select **File | Save As**. Change the **File name** to **Typing extra** and click **Save**.

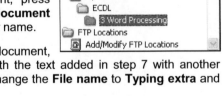

i *To save the document with the same name, to the same location, without displaying any dialog box, click **Save**, or use the key press <Ctrl S>.*

Driving Lesson 11 - Closing a Document/Word

P Park and Read

To clear all text from the screen and begin working on a new document, the current document can be closed. If the document has not been previously saved, or if it has been modified in any way since it was last saved, a prompt to save it will appear. You do not have to close *Word* to close a document, but you should close the application when you've finished working with it.

Manoeuvres

1. The text of **Typing extra** that was saved earlier should still be present on the screen. Move to the bottom of the document, press <**Enter**> twice and type in today's date.

2. Now select the **File** menu and choose the **Close** command. The following message appears:

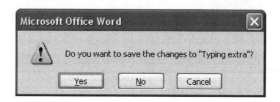

3. Three options are given:

    Yes   Automatically saves the document before clearing it from the window (displays the **Save As** dialog box if the document has just been created).

    No   clears the document from the active window, any changes or additions to the document are lost.

    Cancel   returns to the document.

4. Select **Yes**. Try typing in some text. Nothing happens because no documents are open at the moment.

    When a single document is open, it can be closed using the **Close** button, ☒, at the right of the **Menu Bar**. When more than one document is open, use the **Close** button, ☒, to the right of the **Title Bar**.

5. To close *Word*, select the **File** menu and click **Exit**.

    You can also close Word by clicking the **Close** button at the right of the **Title Bar** and with the key press <**Alt F4**>. If any documents are still open, you will be prompted to save them.

Driving Lesson 12 - Creating a New Document

▣ Park and Read

A new document can be opened at any time within *Word*. There are templates to create a blank document, or various other types of document.

Manoeuvres

1. Select **File | New**. The **New Document Task Pane** appears. There is an option to create a blank document or a new document can be created from a template or from an existing document. To see the available templates click **On my computer**.

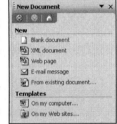

ℹ️ *A new, blank document can also be opened immediately by clicking the **New Blank Document** button,* *, on the*

***Standard Toolbar**.*

2. Make sure the **General** tab is selected. This shows **Blank Document**, **XML Document**, **Web Page** and **E-**

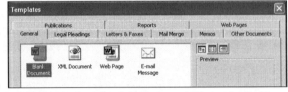

mail Message icons. Click **OK** with the **Blank Document** icon selected to start a blank document. Close this document <u>without</u> saving.

3. Display the **Templates** dialog box again, to view the available templates to base your document on.

4. Select the **Letters & Faxes** tab, click on the **Contemporary Fax** (notice the preview), clicking **OK** would open the template and create a document based on that template with clear instructions on how and where to enter text, similar to most templates.

5. Select the **Memos** tab, click on the **Contemporary Memo** (notice the preview), clicking **OK** would open the template and create a document based on that template.

6. Select the **Other Documents** tab and click on **Agenda Wizard**. Click **OK** to start to create an **Agenda** document using this wizard.

7. Proceed through the wizard making selections from the options provided. Click **Finish** when complete. A document is created based on your selections.

8. Use **File | Close** to clear the document from the screen. Do <u>not</u> save any changes.

Driving Lesson 13 - Open an Existing Document

🅿 Park and Read

An existing document can be opened at any time, to view or amend.

🗘 Manoeuvres

1. The text area of the screen should be clear from the end of the previous Driving Lesson. If not, clear it now by closing any open documents.

2. Select **File | Open**.

ℹ️ *Clicking the **Open** button, 📂, on the **Standard Toolbar** will also display the **Open** dialog box. Alternatively use the key press <**Ctrl O**>.*

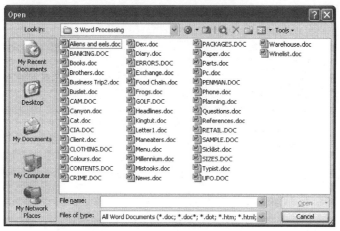

3. **Look in** should show the folder containing the data files, if not, select **My Documents | CIA DATA FILES | ECDL | 3 Word Processing**, or a different location, if appropriate.

4. Select the document **Warehouse** and then click **Open**. A document can also be opened by double clicking on its name.

5. Use **File | Close** to clear the document from the screen.

6. Select **File** from the **Menu Bar**. The last four documents that have been used by *Word* are listed at the bottom of the menu.

ℹ️ *The last four documents are shown by default. More, or less, may be shown if the settings have been changed.*

7. Click once on the file name **Typing** to open the file, then close it again.

Driving Lesson 14 - Views

▣ Park and Read

When working in *Word* there are many different ways to view a document. The most commonly used are **Normal View, Print Layout View** and **Print Preview**. There is also a **Web Layout View** and an **Outline View**. You can easily switch between the different views.

☞ Manoeuvres

1. Open the document **Warehouse**. This document is in **Normal View**, showing the document in its basic format.

2. Change to **Print Layout View** by selecting **View | Print Layout**. In **Print Layout View** the document is shown exactly as it will appear when it is printed. The most obvious difference in this view from **Normal View** is that the document margins can be seen.

3. Change to **Print Preview** by selecting **File | Print Preview**. In **Print Preview**, entire pages and/or multiple pages can be viewed. This view is used to check document layout and pagination.

> **i** *Print Preview can also be selected by clicking the **Print Preview** button, 🔍, from the **Standard Toolbar**.*

4. Select **View | Normal**. There are also buttons at the bottom left of the screen to select views.

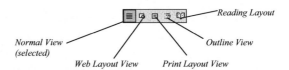

5. Starting with the button at the left, click each of the buttons in turn to see the different views, selecting **Reading Layout** last.

> **i** *This view hides all toolbars apart from **Reading Layout** and **Reviewing**. It is designed for reading documents easily and does not represent how the document would look when printed. Documents can still be edited in this view.*

6. Click 🔲 Close and switch to **Normal View**.

7. Use **File | Close** to close the document <u>without</u> saving. An empty area with no open documents should be on the screen.

Driving Lesson 15 - Saving in Different Formats

Park and Read

Although the usual format for saving documents is as a **Word Document** (with a **.doc** file extension), it is possible to save them in many different formats. A document can be saved as **Plain Text** (with a **.txt** file extension). This means that all formatting, styles and graphics are removed, reducing the file to the simplest text format, which will be recognised by all word processing software. To save in a format that can be read by any version of *Word*, save in **Rich Text Format** (**.rtf** file extension). Documents can also be saved with a format specific to a particular type of software, such as *WordPerfect*.

Manoeuvres

1. Open the document **Scents**. Select **File | Save As**.

2. From the **Save in** box, select the location where the data files are saved. Change the **File name** to **Aromas**.

3. Click the drop down arrow from the **Save as type** box and view the various options and their file name extensions, e.g. **Rich Text Format (*.rtf)**, **Word 6.0/95 (*.doc)**, etc.

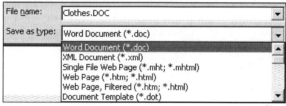

Document extensions, shown above, may not be shown on your computer.

4. Scroll down the list and select **Plain Text (*.txt)**. The file name will change to **Aromas.txt**.

5. Click **Save** and if a dialog box appears about loss of formatting, click **OK**.

6. With the document still open select **File | Save As**. In the data file location, save the document with a **File name** of **Best smells** and select the **Rich Text Format (*.rtf)** file type.

7. **Save** and then close the document.

8. Click **Open**, and ensure **Look in** shows the location of the data files.

9. From **Files of type**, select **All Files**. Select **Aromas** and then **Open**.

10. Notice how the font has changed, then close the document. Open **Best smells** and notice how the **Rich Text Format** has been kept.

11. To save this document with a file extension specific to *WordPerfect*, select **File | Save As** and change the name to **WordPerfect**.

12. Select the file type **WordPerfect 5.0** and click **Save**. If a message about loss of formatting appears, click **Yes** and close the document.

Driving Lesson 16 - Saving as a Template

Park and Read

If a standard document is to be used many times, it can be saved as a **Template** (**.dot** file extension).

Manoeuvres

1.   Open the document **Winelist**. To save this as a **Template**, because its basic format can be used repeatedly when stock changes, select **File | Save As**.

2.   From save as type, select **Document Template**. Notice the folder change in the **Save in** box.

3.   Change the **File name** to **Beverages**. Click **Save** to save the document. Close the document.

4.   To see the new template, select **File | New** and then **On my Computer** from the **Task Pane**.

5.   Click the **General** tab. The new template is displayed as an icon.

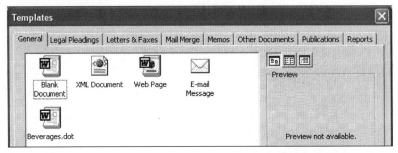

6.   Double click the icon to open a document based on the template. Note that the name on the **Title Bar** is not **Beverages**, but **Document....**

7.   Close the document. The template is to be deleted, so that this Driving Lesson can be performed again on the same PC.

8.   Select **File | New** and select **On my Computer**. Click with the right mouse button on the **Beverages** icon.

9.   Select **Delete** from the menu, choosing **Yes** at the prompt.

Take great care when deleting templates. Make sure that the correct one is deleted.

10. Click **Cancel** to close the **Templates** dialog box.

Driving Lesson 17 - Saving in Earlier Versions

 Park and Read

Documents can be saved in earlier versions of the word processing software to enable users to open documents that do not have the access to the version that the document was produced in, e.g. users of Word 95 cannot open documents produced in Word XP. In this case documents can be saved in earlier version formats that can be used. Some of the formatting and features used may be lost because the older software does not support them.

Manoeuvres

1. Open the file **Winelist**.

2. Select **File | Save As**.

3. From the **Save in** box, select the location where the data files are saved. Change the **File name** to **Winelist2**.

4. Click the drop down arrow from the **Save as type** box and view the various options and their file name extensions.

5. Scroll down the list to view all the different *Word* formats.

6. Select **Word 6.0/95 (*.doc)**.

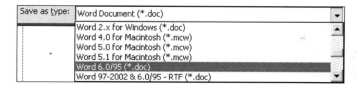

Document extensions, shown above, may not be shown on your computer.

7. Click **Save**.

8. Click **Yes** to convert the file and if a dialog box appears about loss of formatting, click **OK**.

9. Close the document.

Driving Lesson 18 - Revision

This covers the features introduced in this section. Try not to refer to the preceding Driving Lessons while completing it.

1. Open the document named **Crime**.

2. Change to **Print Layout View**.

3. At the end of the document, start a new line and press <Enter> again to create a new paragraph.

4. Add the following sentence as a new paragraph: **This man is a major suspect**.

5. Save a new version of this document - select **File | Versions** and click **Save Now**.

6. Save this version as **Suspect**.

7. Close the document.

8. Open the document named **Brothers**, using the **Open** button.

9. Go to the end of the document and start a new line.

10. Press <Enter> again to leave a blank line after the last paragraph.

11. Type your name and the date, then save the document with a new name - **Brothers2**.

12. Close the document.

13. Reopen **Brothers2** from the list of most recently used documents at the bottom of the **File** menu.

14. Notice that your name and the date have been saved on this document.

15. Close the document.

If you experienced any difficulty completing the Revision, refer back to the Driving Lessons in this section. Then redo the Revision.

Driving Lesson 19 - Revision

This covers the features introduced in this section. Try not to refer to the preceding Driving Lessons while completing it.

1. Open the document **Errors**.

    Save the document in **Plain Text** format, as **Incorrect** then close it.

2. Use the **Elegant Letter** template, found under **On my Computer** within **Letters & Faxes**, to create a new document.

3. Complete the shaded areas where indicated with your own details, but do not enter a job title.

4. Save the document as **Letter**, then add your job title.

5. Save the changes to the document and close it.

6. Start a new document using the **New Blank Document** button, 🗋.

7. Type in this text:

    > **There were many factors that led to the downfall of the French royal family in the late eighteenth century, but perhaps that most often mentioned is the way of life of Queen Marie-Antoinette. Her lavish lifestyle and misunderstanding of the hardships faced by her subjects must have been too much to take for the French peasants, who had no means of feeding themselves or their families.**

8. Ignore any jagged red lines which may appear under any words which are misspelled, for this exercise.

9. Save the document as **Revolution**, then close it and close *Word*.

10. Start *Word* and open the document **Revolution**.

11. Type your name at the bottom of the document then save the changes to the file then close the document **Revolution**.

12. Start a new document.

13. Enter your name on the first line and your address below, using a separate line for each line of your address.

14. Save the document as a template with the file name **Address**.

15. Close all open documents.

If you experienced any difficulty completing the Revision, refer back to the Driving Lessons in this section. Then redo the Revision.

Once you are confident with the features, complete the Record of Achievement Matrix referring to the section at the end of the guide. Only when competent move on to the next Section.

Section 3
Editing Text

By the end of this Section you should be able to:

Insert and Delete Text

Select Words and Sentences

Select Lines and Paragraphs

Insert Special Characters and Symbols

Use Undo and Redo

Show and Hide Non Printing Characters

Insert and Delete Soft Carriage Returns

To gain an understanding of the above features, work through the Driving Lessons in this Section.

For each **Driving Lesson**, read the **Park and Read** instructions, without touching the keyboard, then work through the numbered steps of the **Manoeuvres** on the computer. Complete the **Revision Exercise(s)** at the end of the section to test your knowledge.

Driving Lesson 20 - Inserting and Deleting Text

▣ Park and Read

Both the mouse and the cursor keys can be used to move the insertion point. Mistakes can be erased, or text inserted wherever required.

⌐ Manoeuvres

1. Open the document **Crime**.

2. To erase a mistake, position the insertion point (cursor) to the right of the mistake with the mouse and click. The **<Backspace>** key (a left arrow above **<Enter>**) is used to delete characters to the left. The **<Del>** or **<Delete>** key can be used to delete characters to the right of the cursor. Make the following changes to the text, using the mouse and the keyboard:

3. First paragraph, first sentence: correct **seet** to **seat**.

4. To insert a new paragraph, position the cursor at the end of the first paragraph, last sentence; press <Enter> twice to leave a blank line after the existing paragraph.

5. Type the following text:

   The identity of the murdered woman is not yet known but, at the current stage of the investigation, she is not believed to be the owner of the Fiat.

6. To insert text, position the cursor where the text is required, then type in the text. New characters are inserted to the left of the cursor. Third paragraph, first sentence: insert a space in **62Pinewood Close**.

   On making further enquiries the police discovered that he had been seen several times visiting 62 Pinewood Close, Adamstown with a man in a Mini. On these occasions neighbours remember seeing a red sports car parked outside. Suspicions were aroused as the owner has not been seen there for some time.

7. Fourth paragraph, correct **fond** to **found**.

8. Fifth paragraph, last sentence; delete the **l** in **managled**.

9. Sixth paragraph, insert a space in **nightof**.

10. Sixth paragraph, first sentence; add **his** between **suspicious of** and **story**.

11. To leave the original document unchanged, use **Save As** to save the amended document, changing the **File name** to **Solved** and then close it.

Driving Lesson 21 - Select Words and Sentences

Park and Read

Most features of *Word* work on the basis that text is first selected and an action is then performed upon it. The text, from one character to an entire document, can be selected by clicking and dragging. There are quick key presses for selecting words and sentences.

Manoeuvres

1. Open the document **Banking**. To select the first sentence of the second paragraph, click at the beginning of it, hold down the mouse button and drag to the end of the sentence. The selected text will appear highlighted.

2. To remove the text selection, click once with the mouse away from the selection.

3. Move to the beginning of the title. To select a single character, hold down **<Shift>** and at the same time press the **<→>** key once. Release **<Shift>**. This is easier than using click and drag to select such a small amount of text.

4. To delete words and groups of words, select the text and then press the **<Delete>** key. Using this method, delete the word **Online** in the title.

5. In the first sentence, double click the word **instantly** in **take decisions instantly** to select it, then delete it.

6. In the last sentence, remove the **as** from **are as careful...** add a full stop after **online**. Remove the **,** and delete the rest of the sentence.

Double click on a word to select it.

7. Text can be changed by overtyping. Select the very first sentence, by holding down **<Ctrl>** and clicking once on the sentence.

8. Type in **Online banking lets you manage your money quickly and easily.** The previous text is replaced.

Alternatively, overtyping can also be performed by pressing the <Insert> key to start Overtype Mode. All key presses will then overtype the existing text until the <Insert> key is pressed again to turn it off.

9. Select the first sentence again. Remove the selected text using **<Delete>**. Delete any blank lines.

10. Delete the first sentence of the third paragraph.

11. Close the document <u>without</u> saving the changes.

Driving Lesson 22 - Select Lines and Paragraphs

▣ Park and Read

The **Selection Bar**, an invisible area at the left margin of the page, is used to select larger areas of text. Lines, paragraphs and the entire document can be selected prior to performing further actions, i.e. cut, copy, delete or replace text.

ⓘ *Once text is selected, if any key is pressed, i.e. <Enter>, a, b, etc, the selected text will be deleted and replaced with the key press.*

⌒ Manoeuvres

1. Open the document **Planning**. Select the first line by moving the mouse to the left of the line until it becomes ⌖ and then clicking once.

2. Deselect the text.

3. In the fourth paragraph, remove the sentence beginning **By constant monitoring....**

4. To select a paragraph, position the mouse next to the paragraph to be selected and double click. Remove the whole of the sixth paragraph. Also remove its title and any extra lines.

5. Now paragraph six has been removed, amend the numbering scheme of the remaining paragraphs accordingly.

6. Delete the last but one line of the document.

7. Select the first two paragraphs by clicking and dragging in the **Selection Bar** (⌖).

8. Now delete them.

9. To select an entire document, position the mouse in the **Selection Bar** then treble click. Click in the document to remove the selection.

10. Another method to select an entire document is to hold down <**Ctrl**> and click in the **Selection Bar**. Select the entire document using this method. Delete the whole of the remaining text.

ⓘ *The key press <**Ctrl A**> can also be used to select an entire document.*

11. Close the (empty) document, making sure that the changes are <u>not</u> saved.

Driving Lesson 23 - Symbols

▣ Park and Read

Word has special characters (**Symbols**) that are not available directly from the keyboard. Some situations call for special characters, like ™, © or ®.

☞ Manoeuvres

1. Start a new document.

2. Choose **Insert | Symbol** from the menu to display the **Symbol** dialog box.

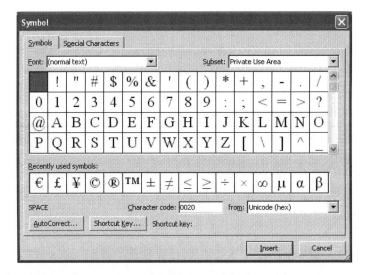

3. With the **Symbols** tab selected, click the drop down arrow associated with **Font**. Change the **Font** to view more symbols. Use the scroll bars to view all the available symbols within a font.

4. To position a symbol in a document at the insertion point, either **double click** the symbol, or click once and then click on **Insert**. Choose **(normal text)** from the list in the **Font** box and, from the symbols displayed, scroll to find ©. Double click the symbol to place it in the document.

5. Now click on 📖 in **Wingdings** and click **Insert**.

6. Select each of the fonts in turn and look at the range of available symbols - there are hundreds. Insert a few.

Driving Lesson 23 - Continued

7.   Within the **Symbol** dialog box, there is an option to select **Special Characters**. Click the **Special Characters** tab. Double click on the **Copyright** character to insert it. Click **Close** to remove the dialog box.

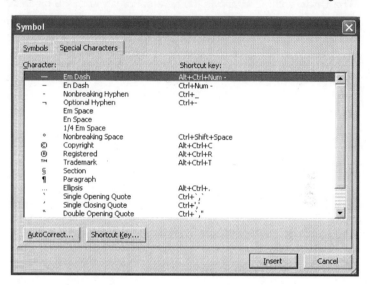

8.   Display the **Symbol** dialog box again and click the **Special Characters** tab. Notice that there is a list of shortcut key presses that can be used to insert certain characters.

9.   Take a note of the key press for a **Trademark** character, ™ then close the dialog box and use the key press to insert it.

10.   Use either method to insert a **Registered** character, ®.

> **i** *To create a key press for a symbol, click the Symbol, then **Shortcut Key**. In the **Customize Keyboard** dialog box enter a key press, e.g. <**Alt T**>, then click **Assign**.*

11.   Close this document <u>without</u> saving and open the document **Sample**.

12.   Replace all the character definitions (in bold) with the symbols themselves.

> **i** *e acute is the é symbol found within (normal text). A bullet can be found within **Symbol**. From the **Font** drop down list, the telephone is found within **Wingdings**.*

13.   Print preview the document.

14.   Save the document as **Sample2** and close it.

Driving Lesson 24 - Undo and Redo

▣ Park and Read

The **Undo** command allows the reversal of some of the last actions performed and **Redo** allows reversal of the **Undo**. These commands, **Undo** ⬚ and **Redo** ⬚, can both be accessed via these buttons on the **Standard Toolbar**.

ℕ Manoeuvres

1.   Open the document **Camera**.

2.   Select and then delete the first sentence.

3.   Oops! That was a mistake. Restore the sentence using **Edit | Undo Clear**.

[i] *The wording after **Undo/Redo** will vary according to the last action performed.*

4.   Now use the **Redo Clear** command to cancel the **Undo**.

5.   Select and delete the second paragraph. Note that the **Redo** button, ⬚, becomes ghosted.

6.   Using the **Undo** button, ⬚, restore the paragraph.

7.   Select **Undo** again to restore the first sentence.

8.   Are you feeling brave? Select the whole document by holding down the <**Ctrl**> key and clicking in the **Selection Bar**, then press <**Delete**>. The whole document should be cleared from the screen.

9.   Choose the **Edit | Undo Clear** command from the **Edit** menu. The document should be restored.

[i] *Select the **Undo**, ⬚, or **Redo**, ⬚, button on the **Standard Toolbar**. If the associated arrow is clicked, then a list of the actions that can be **Undone** or **Redone** appears. To select more than one option, drag down the list. Multiple actions can be undone by clicking the **Undo** button as many times as necessary.*

10. Experiment with **Undo** and **Redo**.

11. Close the document <u>without</u> saving the changes.

Driving Lesson 25 - Show/Hide Characters

▣ Park and Read

The **Show/Hide** feature allows non-printing characters to be viewed on the screen. This includes paragraph marks, tabs, spaces, etc.

> **<Enter>** is shown by the ¶ mark. This is called a paragraph mark or hard carriage return.
>
> A **<Tab>** is shown by the → mark.
>
> Spaces are shown by .... One dot signifies one space.

Viewing these characters can often make manipulating text easier.

Manoeuvres

1. Open the document **Maneaters**.

2. Click the **Show/Hide** button, ¶, on the **Standard Toolbar**.

3. Look for the tab marks, spaces and paragraph marks, as shown in the **Park and Read** information above.

4. At the bottom of the document, type your name and address with **Show/Hide** turned on.

5. Click at the end of your name.

6. Press **<Delete>** to delete the paragraph mark.

7. Notice how the first line of your address now appears immediately after your name. You have merged the paragraphs.

8. Move to page **1** and place the cursor in front of **Sharks have no bone...** in the **Body Form** section.

9. Press **<Enter>** to create a new paragraph.

10. Click the **Show/Hide** button to return the document to normal view.

11. Close the document <u>without</u> saving.

Driving Lesson 26 - Soft Carriage Returns

🄿 Park and Read

A **soft carriage return**, or **line break**, can also be viewed using **Show/Hide** and looks like ↵. Soft carriage returns are used when you want text to appear on two lines, but to be treated as if it were a single line. Another term is **manual line break**. For example, look at the section heading for this section of the guide. This is how it looks in the original document:

> # Section·3↵
> # Editing·Text¶

Because a soft carriage return has been used after the **3**, the two lines are treated as a single line and appear on a single line in the contents list at the front of the guide. Had a hard return been used (like after **Text**), the section heading would have appeared on two lines in the contents.

🄿 Manoeuvres

1. Start a new document and turn on the **Show/Hide** feature.

2. Type in **This demonstrates soft** then press <**Shift Enter**>.

3. The cursor moves to the next line. Type in **carriage returns.**

4. Now press <**Enter**> and type **This demonstrates hard** then press <**Enter**>.

5. Type in **carriage returns**.

6. Place the cursor anywhere in the first line: **This demonstrates soft**.

7. Click the **Center** alignment button, 🖺. Notice how both lines are centred.

8. Now place the cursor within **This demonstrates hard**.

9. Click 🖺. Only the first line is centred because of the hard return.

10. To delete the soft return, position the cursor immediately in front of it and press <**Delete**>.

11. The text is now on one line. Turn off the **Show/Hide** feature.

12. Close the document <u>without</u> saving.

Driving Lesson 27 - Revision

This covers the features introduced in this section. Try not to refer to the preceding Driving Lessons while completing it.

1. Start a new document and type the following letter, using symbols to enter the letters/words in bold type:

    Joe's Car Services
    15 Lincoln Lane
    Sheepfolds
    Norwich
    NC3 1BR

    Today's date

    Dear Mr Hardy

    We have just taken delivery of your new Citroën Saxo and would be pleased if you could call to arrange collection. Please telephone the number below at your convenience.

    Yours sincerely

    Joe Middleton
    Manager
    ☎ 0132 5127719

2. Select the third line of the address, **Sheepfolds** and delete it, as this is incorrect.

3. The telephone area code has changed to **0232**. Make the change.

4. You have just heard that the code has reverted to the original. **Undo** the change.

5. Save the letter as **Delivery** and close it.

If you experienced any difficulty completing the Revision, refer back to the Driving Lessons in this section. Then redo the Revision.

Driving Lesson 28 - Revision

This covers the features introduced in this section. Try not to refer to the preceding Driving Lessons while completing it.

1.   Open **Maneaters**.

2.   Select the first line of text by clicking and dragging.

3.   Click away to deselect the text.

4.   Scroll down the document until you can see the subtitle **Respiration and Circulation**.

5.   Move the cursor to the left of the document. What is this area called?

6.   Select this subtitle using ⇗ .

7.   Deselect the subtitle.

8.   Close **Maneaters** <u>without</u> saving, unless you are continuing with the next revision.

9.   Open the document **Maneaters**, if it is not open already.

10. Go to the paragraph named **Teeth** and select it using ⇗ .

11. Press <**Delete**> to remove the paragraph.

12. Undo the deletion.

13. Position the cursor at the front of the document title and enter **Facts About**.

14. Undo the typing.

15. Redo the typing.

16. Select the whole document and delete it.

17. Undo the deletion.

18. Save the document as **Maneaters2** and close it.

i   *Check the answers at the back of the guide.*

If you experienced any difficulty completing the Revision, refer back to the Driving Lessons in this section. Then redo the Revision.

Driving Lesson 29 - Revision

This covers the features introduced in this section. Try not to refer to the preceding Driving Lessons while completing it.

1. Open the document called **Frogs**.

2. Insert a **soft carriage return** after the words **Common Frog** and before **(Rana temporaria)** so that **(Rana temporaria)** appears on the next line.

3. Centre the text.

4. In the second paragraph, first line, change the word **male** to **female**.

5. In the third paragraph after the sentence ending **do the same lecture next year** insert the following text:

    Unfortunately, they will not be present as two will be on holiday and the other told me he always has to go away at certain times of the year.

6. Insert the special character © below the last paragraph, followed by your name.

7. Save the document as **Lecture** and close it.

8. Open the document **Kingtut**.

9. Turn on the **Show/Hide** feature.

10. In paragraph 2, after the first sentence, enter the following text:

    The dig was funded by Lord Caernarvon, who died shortly after the tomb was opened. Some say this was due to "The Curse of Tutankhamun."

11. Delete the very last sentence.

12. Undo the deletion.

13. Save the amended document as **Kingtut2**.

14. Turn off the **Show/Hide** feature.

15. Close the document.

If you experienced any difficulty completing the Revision, refer back to the Driving Lessons in this section. Then redo the Revision.

Once you are confident with the features, complete the Record of Achievement Matrix referring to the section at the end of the guide. Only when competent move on to the next Section.

Section 4
Printing

By the end of this Section you should be able to:

Preview a Document

Print a Document

Print Parts of a Document

Print Specific Pages

To gain an understanding of the above features, work through the **Driving Lessons** in this **Section**.

For each **Driving Lesson**, read the **Park and Read** instructions, without touching the keyboard, then work through the numbered steps of the **Manoeuvres** on the computer. Complete the **Revision Exercise(s)** at the end of the section to test your knowledge.

Driving Lesson 30 - Previewing a Document

🅿 Park and Read

It is a good idea to check how a document will look before printing it. You can tell if the margins are adequate and if the document looks generally OK using **Print Preview**. Print Preview shows the layout of the document as it will be printed.

Manoeuvres

1. Open the document **Retail**.

2. Press **<Ctrl Page Down>** to move to the second page (check on the status bar that the cursor is within **Page 2**).

3. Select **File | Print Preview**. **Print Preview** contains the following buttons:

Print	🖨	Prints the document.
Magnifier	🔍	Allows any area of the document to be enlarged. Position the mouse over the page. The magnifier will have a + or - it showing zooming in or out. Click the mouse to **Zoom In/Out** of the page.
One Page	🗏	Allows one page to be viewed at a time.
Multiple Pages	🗐	Views as many pages as required (up to 24 pages at once).
Zoom	38% ▾	Adjusts the magnification of the document.
View Ruler	📏	Shows/hides the ruler in **Print Preview**.
Shrink to Fit	🗗	Condenses any document by one page.
Full Screen	🔲	Removes all **Toolbars** and **Menus**.
Close Preview	Close	Returns to **Normal** or **Page Layout** view.

Driving Lesson 30 - Continued

4. Position the mouse over Page 2. A magnifying glass appears, click once. The text should enlarge, click again and it will reduce in size.

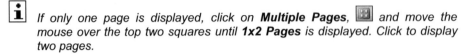 *If only one page is displayed, click on **Multiple Pages**, and move the mouse over the top two squares until **1x2 Pages** is displayed. Click to display two pages.*

5. Position the mouse over Page 1. The magnifying glass is not visible. Click once on the page - the magnifying glass appears. Click once to enlarge the text. Click again.

6. Click the **One Page** button, ▣. Only one page can now be viewed.

7. Experiment using the **<Page Up>** and **<Page Down>** buttons on the keyboard and/or the scroll bars to move through the document (note the appearance of the page numbers while scrolling).

8. Click the arrow associated with **Zoom**. Select **200%**, then **10%**, then **Two Pages**, then **Page Width** and lastly **Whole Page**.

9. Click the **Multiple Pages** button to display a grid of pages. To view all the pages in the document, i.e. 3, click and drag to select the first 3 boxes.

10. Click on **Shrink to Fit**, 📄. The document has been shrunk to fit on to 2 pages!

11. Return to the previous view of your document using **Close**, Close .

12. Close the document <u>without</u> saving to lose the changes.

Driving Lesson 31 - Printing a Document

◨ Park and Read

Once a document has been previewed, it is ready to be printed. Various print options are available, such as printing the entire document, or printing only a few pages.

ℝ Manoeuvres

1.   Open the document **Retail** again. Make sure that the printer is switched on, is connected to the computer and loaded with paper.

2.   To print a copy of the whole document, click **Print**, 🖨, on the toolbar.

3.   Selected pages of a document can also be printed. Add a number to the top of each page manually, then select **File | Print** or use the key press **<Ctrl P>** to display the **Print** dialog box.

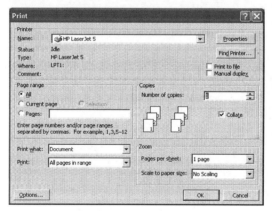

4.   From the **Print** dialog box, locate the **Page range** section and in **Pages** type **2**. In **Number of Copies**, type **3**.

5.   Select **OK** to print **3** copies of page **2**.

6.   Select the first sentence. To print only the selected text, select **File | Print**. Choose the **Selection** option from **Page range** and click **OK**.

ℹ️ *To print current page, i.e. the page the cursor is on, select **Current page**.*

7.   To print pages 2 through to the end of the document using **File | Print** or **<Ctrl P>** and in the **Pages** box in the **Page range** area, type **2-**.

8.   Print pages **1** and **3** only by entering **1,3** in the **Pages** box.

9.   Close the document <u>without</u> saving.

Driving Lesson 32 - Revision

This covers the features introduced in this section. Try not to refer to the preceding Driving Lessons while completing it.

1. What happens if you press ?

2. What is the normal setting for the **Page range**?

3. What is the normal setting for the **Number of copies**?

4. What does **Print Preview** do?

5. Open the document **Canyon**.

6. **Print Preview** the document.

7. Add your name to the end of the document.

8. **Print Preview** the result and print out one copy of the document.

9. Close the document <u>without</u> saving.

10. Open the document **Maneaters**.

11. Type your name at the end.

12. **Print Preview** the document. How many pages does it contain?

13. View the other pages using the **Multiple Pages** button, .

14. Use **<Page Up>** and **<Page Down>** to change the screen display. The selected page is shown in the **Status Bar**.

15. Close **Print Preview** and print only the first page of the document.

16. Close the document <u>without</u> saving.

Check the answers at the back of the guide.

If you experienced any difficulty completing the Revision, refer back to the Driving Lessons in this section. Then redo the Revision.

Driving Lesson 33 - Revision

This covers the features introduced in this section. Try not to refer to the preceding Driving Lessons while completing it.

1.   Open the document **PC** and switch to **Print Layout View**.

2.   Select the title and the first paragraph and print only this selection.

3.   Print page **2** only.

4.   Print pages **3 - 4** only.

5.   Close the document <u>without</u> saving.

6.   Open the document **Golf**.

7.   Preview the document, then print one copy, using a button.

8.   Close **Golf** <u>without</u> saving.

9.   Open the document **Maneaters**.

10.   Type your name and the date at the end of the document

11.   **Print Preview** the document.

12.   Select the section about **Senses**.

13.   Print the selected text only.

14.   Print pages **1** and **3** only with a single action, i.e. do not print page **1** and then open the dialog box again to print page **3**.

15.   Close the document <u>without</u> saving.

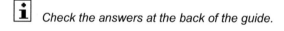 *Check the answers at the back of the guide.*

If you experienced any difficulty completing the Revision, refer back to the Driving Lessons in this section. Then redo the Revision.

Once you are confident with the features, complete the Record of Achievement Matrix referring to the section at the end of the guide. Only when competent move on to the next Section.

Section 5
Formatting Text

By the end of this Section you should be able to:

Underline, Embolden and Italicise Text

Change Fonts and Text Size

Apply Text Effects, Subscript and Superscript

Use the Format Painter

Cut, Copy and Paste

To gain an understanding of the above features, work through the **Driving Lessons** in this **Section**.

For each **Driving Lesson**, read the **Park and Read** instructions, without touching the keyboard, then work through the numbered steps of the **Manoeuvres** on the computer. Complete the **Revision Exercise(s)** at the end of the section to test your knowledge.

Driving Lesson 34 - Underline, Bold and Italic

P Park and Read

As text is entered into a document, it is possible to format it as it is typed. Formatting features can be applied from the keyboard, or by clicking command buttons on the toolbars.

Manoeuvres

1. Select the **New** button, [image], to start a new document.

2. Practise activating the features using the mouse. Click once on the Toolbar buttons, **B** *I* **U**. When a particular feature is in operation, the button on the Toolbar appears to be pressed down. Turn the selected feature off by clicking once more on the button.

3. Practise activating, bold, italic and underline features using the key presses <**Ctrl B**>, <**Ctrl I**> and <**Ctrl U**> respectively. Turn the features off by pressing <**Ctrl Spacebar**>, or repeat the key press.

4. Type in the following text using **Bold**, **Underline** and *Italic*, turning the features on and off as required.

    ### Floppy Disks

    Before a disk can be used it needs to be *formatted* which means that the **tracks** on which the computer stores its data need to be put on the disk. Different computers **format disks** in different ways. Personal computers (PCs) all format disks in the same way, making them compatible with other machines.

    It is easy to damage a disk so be careful. Some of the things that can **cause damage** include exposing the disk to sunlight, magnets or moisture, damaging the casing or touching the inner disk film.

5. When finished, scroll back through the text using the left arrow key. Note that the **Underline**, **Bold** and *Italic* buttons on the toolbar appear pressed at the points where they were activated and normal where they were not.

6. Save the document as **Disks**.

7. Print a copy of the document and then close it.

Driving Lesson 35 - Formatting of Selected Text

▣ Park and Read

Text formats are usually applied after text has been typed. This speeds up text entry and formatting. To change the appearance of text that has already been entered, first select the text using the mouse and then apply the formatting feature.

☞ Manoeuvres

1. Open the document **Parts**.

2. Underline the title and the three sub headings.

3. Change the formatting of the following words to bold:

    First paragraph:　　　**CPU**, **Control Unit**, **Memory**, **ROM**, **RAM**, and **Arithmetic Unit**.

    Second paragraph:　**keyboards**.

    Third paragraph:　　**monitor** (twice).

> **i** *To apply a formatting feature to a single word, position the cursor within the word and apply the required format.*

4. Print the document.

5. Save the document as **Parts2**.

6. Remove the underlining from the title and return the word **keyboards** to its normal appearance.

7. Italicise the word **brain** in the first paragraph by placing the cursor within the word, and then click the **Italic** button.

8. Italicise the whole of the second paragraph.

9. Print out the document.

10. Continue to experiment with the appearance of the document. For instance, try applying several of the formatting features at the same time.

11. Close the document. Do <u>not</u> save the changes.

Driving Lesson 36 - Fonts and Text Size

▣ Park and Read

A font is a type or style of print. Examples of fonts are Courier, Times New Roman, Arial, etc. A combination of the software in use and the selected printer determines which fonts are available for use. You can choose a font before starting to type, or you can select text that has already been entered and then change the font. The size of the font can also be changed. *Word* defines size in **points** - the larger the point size, the larger the character appears.

⬧ Manoeuvres

1. Open the document **Cia** and select the whole of the document.

2. Change the font of the document using the **Font** box, | Times New Roman ▼ |, on the toolbar.

3. Select a different font from the list and add a line at the top of the document stating the chosen font.

4. Print a copy of the text. Repeat for a selection of fonts on the font list. This provides reference documents for the range of fonts available from the selected printer.

> **ℹ** *To change the font of a single word, position the cursor within the word and choose the required font.*

5. Close the document <u>without</u> saving the changes.

6. Open the document **Sizes**. Select each line of text in turn that describes a different size and from the **Size** box, | 12 ▼ |, choose the size that the text describes.

> **ℹ** *To preview text size prior to changing text, select **Format | Font**. The font can also be changed from here. To change the size of a single word, position the cursor within the word and choose a size from the **Size** box.*

7. Try placing the cursor within a word and changing the font size.

8. When all the text has been correctly sized, select **File | Print Preview** to see the result and print a copy of the document.

9. Save the document as **New text sizes**, then close it.

Driving Lesson 37 - Changing Text Appearance

🄿 Park and Read

Different colours can be applied to text, making it more eye-catching. Think carefully, though, before using too much colour. It might make a document more difficult to read, or detract from its purpose.

↱ Manoeuvres

1.   Open the document **Colours**. Select the text **This text is red**.

2.   Select **Format | Font** to display the **Font** dialog box.

3.   Use the **Font Color** drop down list to change the font colour to **red**.

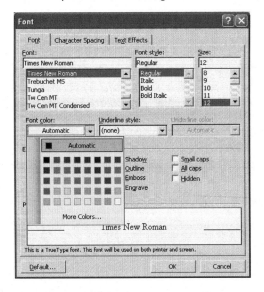

4.   Click **OK**.

5.   Text colour can be changed using the drop down arrow to the right of the **Font Color** button, , on the toolbar. Use the button to change the colour of the next line of text to **blue**.

6.   Change the colour of the remaining text as stated in each line.

7.   Click the **Font Color** button and type your name at the bottom of the document. The text is the same as the colour shown on the button.

8.   Now select **Print Preview** to see the results. If a colour printer is available print a copy of the document.

9.   Save this document as **Colours2**. Close the document.

Driving Lesson 38 - Subscript and Superscript

Park and Read

Superscript and subscript make the text respectively higher or lower than the other text on the same line, e.g. in mathematical or chemical terms.

Manoeuvres

1. Start a new document.

2. Type in the following text: **The chemical symbol for water is H2O.**

3. Select the **2** and then **Format | Font**.

4. Check **Subscript** and click **OK**.

> The chemical symbol for water is H_2O.

5. With the cursor at the end of the sentence, press **<Enter>** and type **43 = 64**.

6. This is obviously incorrect. Select the **3** and then **Format | Font**.

7. Check **Superscript** and then **OK**. The sum is now correct: 4 cubed = 64.

> The chemical symbol for water is H_2O.
> $4^3 = 64$

8. Start a new line and type in the following text: **1st 2nd 3rd 4th 5th** .Notice how the superscript feature is automatically activated by *Word*.

9. Close the document <u>without</u> saving.

Driving Lesson 39 - Changing Case

▣ Park and Read

Four different character cases can be used within *Word*. These are:

Sentence Case	the first letter of the sentence is in upper case.
Lowercase	all the letters are in small case.
Uppercase	all the letters are capitalised.
Title Case	all words begin with an uppercase letter.

There is a fifth option:

tOGGLE cASE	that converts every character to the opposite of what it is, lowercase to uppercase and vice-versa.

⟳ Manoeuvres

1. In a new document, type **the bus was late every morning**. Notice that the first letter is capitalised automatically.

2. Select the text, then select **Format | Change Case** to display the **Change Case** dialog box.

3. Select **UPPERCASE**.

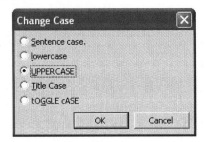

4. Click **OK** to capitalise the text.

5. With the text selected, press **<Shift F3>** to change the case to **lowercase**.

i *The key press <Shift F3> rotates between **UPPERCASE**, **lowercase** and **Title Case**.*

6. Press **<Shift F3>** again to change the text to **Title Case**.

i *The menu command **Format | Change Case | tOGGLE cASE** reverses the current case settings.*

7. Close the document <u>without</u> saving.

Driving Lesson 40 - Format Painter

🅿 Park and Read

Once part of a document has been formatted you may wish to use the same format on another part of a document. This can be done using the **Format Painter**, which will copy the formatting applied to the original text and apply it to other text.

Manoeuvres

1. Open the document **Scents** and select the first paragraph. Make it underlined, bold and change the **Font** to any other.

2. With the newly formatted paragraph selected, from the **Standard Toolbar**, click the **Format Painter** button, 🖌. The mouse pointer changes to a paintbrush 🖌I .

3. Click and drag to select the second paragraph. Once the mouse has been released, the paragraph will be formatted in the same manner.

ⓘ *To format more than one selection, **double click** the **Format Painter** button. This will allow text to be selected in several different areas of the document. Click the **Format Painter** button again, or press the <**Esc**> key to turn it off.*

4. The mouse pointer returns to its normal state, **Format Painter** is turned off.

5. Close the document <u>without</u> saving.

Driving Lesson 41 - Cut, Copy and Paste

▣ Park and Read

The **Cut**, **Copy** and **Paste** commands allow text to be moved around a document, from one place to another, quickly and easily. When text is cut, it is removed from its original location; when copied, the original is untouched. When copied or cut, text is placed in a temporary storage area known as the **Clipboard**. Up to **24** cut or copied items can be held on the **Clipboard**.

↱ Manoeuvres

1. Open the document **Planning**. To view the **Clipboard Task Pane** select **Edit | Office Clipboard**. Because the **Clipboard** is shared between all *Office* applications, there may already be some items on it. If so, click the **Clear All** button, [✗ Clear All].

2. Highlight the title **Production Planning** and its associated paragraph. Select **Edit | Cut** command.

3. To place the paragraph of text from the **Clipboard** at the end of the document, move the cursor to the correct position, press <**Enter**> as required to separate the paragraphs and use **Edit | Paste**.

ⓘ *Cut, Copy and Paste buttons,* [✂ 🗐 🗐]*, are on the toolbar. Quick key presses: Cut <**Ctrl** **X**>, Copy <**Ctrl** **C**>, Paste <**Ctrl** **V**>.*

4. Create another new line at the end of the document, then click the paragraph as it appears on the **Clipboard Task Pane**. This also pastes the paragraph into the document. Undo the last action.

5. Highlight paragraph number 7, including its title. Click **Copy**, [🗐] and this item appears on the **Clipboard**, next to the item cut earlier.

6. Paste paragraph 7 at the top of the document, ignore any **Smart Tag** that may appear, then delete the original paragraph.

7. Use the **Cut, Copy** and **Paste** commands to reverse the order of the paragraphs so that the order reads 7, 6, 5, 4, 3, 2, 1. Delete the paragraph numbers and space the paragraphs as necessary.

8. Use the **Cut, Copy** and **Paste** buttons on the toolbar to order the paragraphs alphabetically by their title name, then clear the **Clipboard** and close it.

9. Save the document as **Planning2** and close it.

Driving Lesson 42 - Revision

This covers the features introduced in this section. Try not to refer to the preceding Driving Lessons while completing it.

1. What effects do the following buttons have if they are clicked when text is selected:

    a) **B** ?   b) *I* ?   c) **U** ?

2. What is a **Font**? Which menu command displays the **Font** dialog box?

3. Name two ways to change the colour of text.

4. Open the document **Food Chain** and apply **Bold** and **Underline** formatting to the title.

5. Apply **Italic** formatting to the words **An example is:**

6. Apply **Bold** formatting to the line **Dandelion - rabbit - fox** and insert a blank line below it.

7. Apply **Italic** formatting to the words **Other examples of food chains are:**.

8. Apply **Bold** formatting to the remaining three lines of text and insert blank lines between them.

9. Print one copy of the document and then close it <u>without</u> saving.

10. Open the document **Maneaters**. Change the font size of the title to **26pt**.

11. Change the size of the subheadings to **18pt**, and change the remaining text to **14pt**.

12. Make the following colour changes:

    Introduction heading and text - **Dark Red**

    Body Form heading and text - **Teal**

    Respiration and Circulation heading and text - **Pink**

    Teeth heading and text - **Bright Green**

    Diet heading and text - **Orange**

    Methods of Reproduction heading and text - **Dark Blue**

    Senses heading and text - **Gold**

    Conclusion heading and text - **Red**

13. Change the font of the title to **Tahoma**.

14. Select the entire document and change the colour to **Automatic**.

15. Print a single copy of the document, then close it <u>without</u> saving.

Check the answers at the back of the guide.

If you experienced any difficulty completing the Revision, refer back to the Driving Lessons in this section. Then redo the Revision.

Driving Lesson 43 - Revision

This covers the features introduced in this section. Try not to refer to the preceding Driving Lessons while completing it.

1. Open the document **Exchange** and print one copy.

2. Ensure that the **Clipboard** toolbar is visible.

3. If appropriate, clear any existing content from the **Clipboard**.

4. Select the third paragraph beginning **We will be visiting interesting sites...** and **Copy** the text.

5. **Paste** the text so that it becomes the second paragraph.

6. Delete the copied paragraph from its original position.

7. Ensure that the spacing between paragraphs is correct.

8. Select the final paragraph; **The following staff...** and **Cut** the text.

9. **Paste** the text so that it becomes the fourth paragraph.

10. Print a copy of the document in its current form.

11. Ensure that the **Clipboard** is cleared, select the first paragraph and **Cut** it.

12. Select and **Cut** each of the remaining paragraphs in turn until the document has no text left in it.

13. Use the **Clipboard** to **Paste** the paragraphs back to their original positions.

14. Close the document <u>without</u> saving.

If you experienced any difficulty completing the Revision, refer back to the Driving Lessons in this section. Then redo the Revision.

Driving Lesson 44 - Revision

This covers the features introduced in this section. Try not to refer to the preceding Driving Lessons while completing it.

1. Open the document **Sicklist**. Use the **Cut** and **Paste** command to put each employee's record in ascending alphabetical order, by surname.

2. Make the first six names bold and green, the second six italic and pink and the last six underlined and blue. Change the font of all the text to **Tahoma 9pt** (use a different font if necessary).

3. Print the document, copy the records and paste them at the end of the document. Change the font of the last two copied records to **Arial** and make them violet and bold.

4. Use the **Format Painter** to apply this formatting to the remainder of the list, then close the document <u>without </u>saving.

5. Clear and remove the **Clipboard** and open the document **Penman**.

6. Move the last sentence of the third paragraph beginning **If you are interested**, to form a new last paragraph.

7. Add in the telephone number **Tel.: (0191) 549 5002** between the address and the date. Adjust the spacing as appropriate.

8. Highlight the text **Penman Walker** and **The world's first robotic dog walker**. Embolden the selected text using the button on the Toolbar.

9. Underline **VERY** in at **VERY low cost** and italicise the word **PENMAN** in the third paragraph.

10. Select all of the text and change the font and size.

11. Select **Penman Walker** and use **Format | Font** to change its size to **20**.

12. Save the document using the filename **Penman2**.

13. Print a copy of the document, then close it.

If you experienced any difficulty completing the Revision, refer back to the Driving Lessons in this section. Then redo the Revision.

Once you are confident with the features, complete the Record of Achievement Matrix referring to the section at the end of the guide. Only when competent move on to the next Section.

Section 6
Tools

By the end of this Section you should be able to:

Check Spelling

Hyphenate Text

Search for Text

Replace Text

Use the Zoom Control

Change Preferences

To gain an understanding of the above features, work through the **Driving Lessons** in this **Section**.

For each **Driving Lesson**, read the **Park and Read** instructions, without touching the keyboard, then work through the numbered steps of the **Manoeuvres** on the computer. Complete the **Revision Exercise(s)** at the end of the section to test your knowledge.

Driving Lesson 45 - Spelling Checker

▣ Park and Read

Word comes with a large dictionary, to help you check spelling in a document. Proper names and places can be added to a supplementary dictionary. There are two main ways of spell checking. Either spell check while typing, or use the **Spelling and Grammar Checker**. This feature allows you to delete repeated words as well as correct spelling errors.

ⓘ *To check spelling while typing, select* **Tools | Options** *and the* **Spelling & Grammar** *tab. Make sure* **Check spelling as you type** *is selected and click* **OK**. *Unrecognised words will be underlined in red as soon as they are entered.*

⌐ Manoeuvres

1. Open the document **UFO**. Add a title **UFO** in bold.

2. With the cursor at the top of the document, check for spelling errors and deal with them accordingly, by using the **Spell Checker** button, 🔲 (**Tools | Spelling and Grammar** or <F7> can also be used). Remove the check from **Check grammar**.

3. The first word to be highlighted is **aproached**. From the **Suggestions**, select **approached** and click on **Change** (**Change All** will change each occurrence of the word in the document). Continue in this way, dealing with each selected word, choosing whether to change, ignore, delete, etc. as required. When a 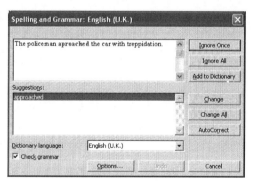 repeated word is encountered, a **Delete** option will appear. Click this to remove one of the repeated words.

ⓘ *Notice the* **Spell Book** *on the* **Status Bar**. *This indicates the current status of the document. If there are mistakes,* 🔲 *appears; if everything is correct,* 🔲 *appears. Double clicking on the book will display a short menu providing alternatives for a single spelling error. Right clicking an incorrectly spelled word will also produce a list of suggested alternatives.*

4. When the **Spelling and Grammar** check is complete, click **OK**.

5. Obtain a printed copy of the document. Close without saving.

Driving Lesson 46 - Add to Dictionary

▣ Park and Read

Some words and proper names are not recognised automatically by *Word*. To prevent these being marked as an error each time, they can be added to the dictionary. After these words have been added, they won't appear again as errors.

⟲ Manoeuvres

1. Open the document **Maneaters**.

2. Select **Tools | Spelling and Grammar**. Move the dialog box if necessary.

3. Ensure the **Check grammar** box is <u>not</u> ticked. The first error found is a spelling.

4. Click **Ignore Once** to ignore the title of the document. The next error is highlighted.

5. **Catshark** is a proper name. Click **Add to Dictionary** to add the word to the dictionary.

ℹ *If someone else has worked through this Driving Lesson on your computer, the word may already be in the dictionary, as it can only be added once.*

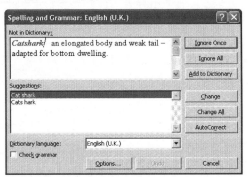

6. All the remaining words are zoological terms or names. **Add** them all to the dictionary.

7. Click **OK** when the spelling check complete message appears and move to the end of the document.

8. To ensure the dictionary has been updated type the following words: **oophagy**, **denticles** and **swellshark**.

9. Notice how the words are not underlined.

10. Leave the document open.

Driving Lesson 47 - Hyphenation

▣ Park and Read

Hyphens help to remove surplus space from justified text and narrow columns by splitting words on to two lines. Hyphenation can be applied to documents manually or automatically. If you choose to hyphenate automatically, *Word* decides where to place the hyphens; if you choose manual hyphenation, then you can accept or reject each hyphenation suggested.

☞ Manoeuvres

1.   Use the document **Maneaters** and make sure it is in **Print Layout** view. This document is **justified** – it has straight left and right margins.

2.   Move to the beginning of the document.

3.   Select **Tools | Language | Hyphenation**.

4.   From the **Hyphenation** dialog box, check the **Automatically hyphenate document** option.

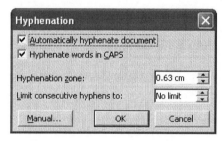

5.   Click **OK** and scroll through the document to see where the hyphens have been added.

6.   Click **Undo** to cancel the hyphenation then select **Tools | Language | Hyphenation** again.

7.   Click the **Manual** button to perform the hyphenation manually. The first suggested hyphenation is displayed.

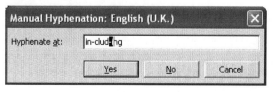

8.   Click **Yes** to accept the hyphenation. Reject all the remaining suggestions until hyphenation is complete, then click **OK**.

9.   Close the document <u>without</u> saving.

Driving Lesson 48 - Searching a Document

🄿 Park and Read

Visually searching for a character, word or phrase in a document can be tedious. The **Find** command moves directly to a specific word or string of characters. You can search for every occurrence of a specified word or phrase.

🄿 Manoeuvres

1.   Open the document **Golf**.

2.   Select **Edit | Find**. The **Find and Replace** dialog box is then displayed.

> 🄸 *To view the **Find and Replace** dialog box press <Ctrl F>, or click ⊙ (vertical scroll bar near the bottom) and then click 🏛.*

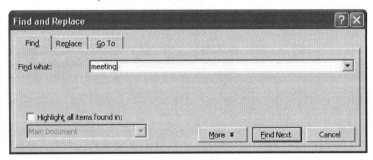

3.   Enter the word **meeting** in the **Find what** box.

4.   Click **Find Next** to begin the search. If a match is found, the word is highlighted.

5.   Keep clicking **Find Next** to find all occurrences of the word.

6.   When all occurrences have been found a message is displayed. Click **OK** to end the search.

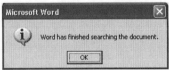

7.   To search for a phrase, in **Find what** delete the existing text and type **delay the appointment**.

8.   Click **Find Next**. The requested phrase is found in the last paragraph.

9.   Click **Cancel** and leave the document open.

Driving Lesson 49 - Replace

▣ Park and Read

The **Replace** facility works in a similar way to **Find**; it gives the option to exchange each chosen occurrence of a character, word or phrase with an alternative.

ℝ Manoeuvres

1. Use the document **Golf**. To replace the name **Bloomfield** with **Broomfield**, place the cursor at the beginning of the document and select **Edit | Replace**.

ⓘ *Pressing <Ctrl H> will also open the Find and Replace dialog box.*

2. Enter **Bloomfield** in the **Find what** box and **Broomfield** in **Replace with** box.

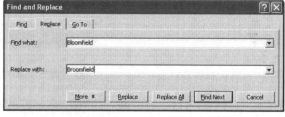

3. Select **Find Next** to identify the first occurrence of the name then click **Replace**. Click **OK** at the end of the search.

4. Replace the phrase **Finance and General Purposes Committee** with **Golf Club Directors'** automatically, by entering the first phrase in the **Find what** box and the second in the **Replace with** box and then clicking **Replace All**.

5. Click **OK** when the message opposite appears and close the **Replace** dialog box by clicking on **Close**.

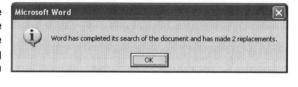

6. Use **Find** to check the changes. Save the document as **Golf2** and close it.

7. Open the document **Exchange**. The exchange trip is actually between France and the US. All instances of **£** must be replaced with **$**.

8. Select **Edit | Replace**. In **Find what** enter **£** and in **Replace with** enter **$** (the dollar sign can be found above the number keys. Even if there is only a Euro symbol, **€**, holding down **<Shift>** while pressing the key will still create a dollar sign).

9. Click **Replace All** and click **OK** at the completed search message.

10. Save the document as **American Exchange** and close it.

Driving Lesson 50 - Zoom Control

▣ Park and Read

Zoom Control is a facility, which allows a document to be viewed in various magnifications. It will allow the document to be reduced or increased in size thus allowing more or less of a document to be displayed on screen.

⌐ Manoeuvres

1. Open the document **Retail**. In **Print Layout** view, select **View | Zoom**.

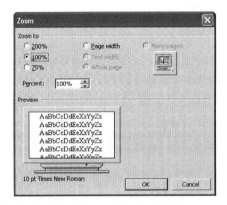

2. Select the **Whole page** option under **Zoom to** and click **OK** to see the effect. Select **View | Zoom** again and try some of the other options.

3. In the **Zoom** dialog box, click the button next to **Many pages**. Notice the available options. Using these settings several pages could be viewed on screen at the same time.

4. Change the zoom to **100%**. Click **OK** to change the view of the document.

5. The drop down list on the **Standard Toolbar**, [100% ▾], can also be used to set the zoom percentage. Select **25%** then **200%**.

6. Try out a few more options then return the setting to **100%** and close the document <u>without</u> saving.

ℹ️ *Once the **Zoom Control** has been altered, the chosen view will be the default view for all **New** documents.*

Driving Lesson 51 - Preferences

Park and Read

Basic options (**preferences**) can be set in *Word*, for example the user name, which is automatically added to certain templates. By default documents are opened from and saved to the **My Documents** folder. These default locations can also be changed.

Manoeuvres

1. Close *Word* and then start *Word* again. This is so the default settings can be seen. Click ☐ and notice that **Look in** in the **Open** dialog box shows **My Documents**.

    i   *Because you have been opening data files from the 3 **Word Processing** folder, this would have been the default folder if the program had not been closed in step 1.*

2. Click **Cancel** to close the dialog box and click ☐. The **Save As** dialog box also saves by default to **My Documents**. Click **Cancel**.

3. To change this file location, select **Tools | Options** and the **File Locations** tab. Make sure **Documents** is selected from **File types**.

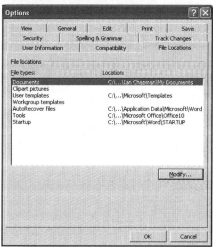

4. Click **Modify**. To open and save on the **Desktop**, click the **Desktop** button from the **Places Bar**, ☐.

Driving Lesson 51 - Continued

 *A different folder could have been selected from* **Look in**.

5.   Click **OK** and **OK** again.

6.   Click 🖼. Notice how **Look in** shows the **Desktop**.

| Look in: | 🖼 Desktop | ▼ |

7.   Click **Cancel**. Check the **Save As** dialog box to see where the document would be saved to.

8.   **Cancel** the dialog box.

9.   To change the file locations back to **My Documents** select **Tools | Options** and the **File Locations** tab.

10. With **Documents** selected, click **Modify** and select **My Documents** from the **Places Bar**.

11. Click **OK** and select the **User Information** tab.

12. To change the user details enter your own name in **Name** and your initials in **Initials**.

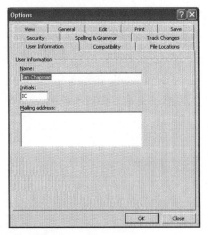

13. Click **OK** and start a new document.

14. Select **File | Properties** and the **Summary** tab. Notice how your name is shown as the **Author**. Click **Cancel.**

15. **Close all** open documents <u>without</u> saving.

Driving Lesson 52 - Revision

This covers the features introduced in this section. Try not to refer to the preceding Driving Lessons while completing it.

1. Open the document **Mistooks**, how many possible spelling errors are identified?

2. Ensure that the cursor is at the beginning of the document and start the **Spelling and Grammar Checker**.

3. Use the **Spelling and Grammar Checker** to correct any mistakes.

4. Use the **Replace** facility to change the word **cheering** to **pleasant**.

5. Using **Replace**, change **lottery** to **Lotto**.

6. Ensure that the cursor is at the beginning of the document.

7. Use the **Find** facility to find the first occurrence of the word **probability**.

8. How many times can **Find Next** be clicked before the search finishes?

9. Close the document <u>without</u> saving changes.

10. Open the document **Phone**.

11. Change to **Print Layout View** and change the **Zoom** to **150%**.

12. Underline the title.

13. Change the **Zoom** to **100%**.

14. Read the document through. How many words have jagged red lines below them?

15. Check the document for spelling. Correct the errors found.

16. The spelling checker does not find the irregular case of **DO** at the start of the last sentence or **contract** which should be **contact**. Make these changes manually.

17. Obtain a printed copy of **Phone**, and close it <u>without</u> saving.

18. Open the document **Kingtut**.

19. Apply automatic hyphenation to the document.

20. Print the document.

21. Close it <u>without</u> saving.

 Check the answers at the back of the guide.

If you experienced any difficulty completing the Revision, refer back to the Driving Lessons in this section. Then redo the Revision.

Driving Lesson 53 - Revision

This covers the features introduced in this section. Try not to refer to the preceding Driving Lessons while completing it.

1. Open the document **Cat**.

2. Replace all occurrences of the name **Wanda** with **Wilma**.

3. Replace all occurrences of the name **Pyewacket** with **Grimalkin**.

4. Apply automatic hyphenation to the document.

5. Add your name to the end of the text.

6. Print a single copy of the document.

7. Close it <u>without</u> saving.

8. Start a new document.

 *A document (even a blank document) must be open for **Tools | Options** to be available.*

9. Change the location from which files are opened by default to the **3 Word Processing** folder (see **Downloading the Data Files** on page 4 for the location).

10. Check that the preferences have been changed by clicking the **Open** button.

11. Change the default open location back to **My Documents**.

12. Close any open documents <u>without</u> saving.

If you experienced any difficulty completing the Revision, refer back to the Driving Lessons in this section. Then redo the Revision.

Once you are confident with the features, complete the Record of Achievement Matrix referring to the section at the end of the guide. Only when competent move on to the next Section.

Section 7
Formatting Paragraphs

By the end of this Section you should be able to:

Align Text

Indent Paragraphs

Apply Advanced Indentation

Apply Bullets and Numbers

Change Line and Paragraph Spacing

Apply and Change Tab Settings

Change Tab Alignment

Apply Borders

To gain an understanding of the above features, work through the **Driving Lessons** in this **Section**.

For each **Driving Lesson**, read the **Park and Read** instructions, without touching the keyboard, then work through the numbered steps of the **Manoeuvres** on the computer. Complete the **Revision Exercise(s)** at the end of the section to test your knowledge.

Driving Lesson 54 - Alignment

🅿 Park and Read

Alignment refers to where text appears on each line in relation to the margins. Word is capable of four types of text alignment: **Left** - straight left margin, uneven right margin, **Centred** - aligned with the centre of the page, **Right** - uneven left margin, straight right margin and **Justified** - straight left and right margins. It's often a matter of preference which alignment you use, but justified text looks much neater.

☞ Manoeuvres

1. Open the document **Cia**.

2. Embolden **quality** in the first paragraph and the names of the directors in the same paragraph. Alignment selection is made by selecting the alignment buttons which are found on the toolbar.

Align Left ———   ——— *Justify*

Center   *Align Right*

ℹ️ *Depending on the customisation of individual PCs, the buttons may not appear together as in the diagram above.*

ℹ️ *The* **Format | Paragraph | Indents and Spacing | Alignment** *command contains the options for controlling text alignment.*

3. Highlight the first paragraph. Click the **Justify** button, 🔲. Note that the text now has straight right and left margins.

4. If only one paragraph is to be aligned, the insertion point need only to be placed in the paragraph, for the effect to take place. Position the cursor within the second paragraph. Right align the text by clicking 🔲.

5. Click in the third paragraph and click the **Center** button, 🔲. The text is aligned about the centre of each line.

6. With the cursor in the same paragraph, click the **Left** button, 🔲. The text returns to its default, left alignment.

7. Print out a copy of the text. Close the document <u>without</u> saving any changes.

Driving Lesson 55 - Indenting Paragraphs

▣ Park and Read

An indented paragraph is one where the left edge of the text is further from the margin than the other paragraphs. It is possible to indent the first line of a paragraph by a different amount to the rest of the paragraph (see next Driving Lesson). The **<Tab>** key is used to indent just the first line of a paragraph, but the **Increase Indent** button, ▦, on the toolbar is used to indent a whole paragraph. Each time the button is pressed, the paragraph is indented to the next tab stop. As good practice, default indents (or the **<Tab>** key) should be used to indent paragraphs properly and consistently - do not use the spacebar to do this.

⟳ Manoeuvres

1. Open the document **Warehouse**.

2. Fully justify the second paragraph.

3. Indent the third and fourth paragraphs to the first tab stop by selecting them and using the **Increase Indent** button, ▦.

i *Click the **Indent** button as many times as necessary to indent the paragraph by the required amount.*

4. Place the insertion point in the third paragraph and click the **Decrease Indent** button, ▦, to remove the indentation.

i *Increase Indent <**Ctrl M**>. Decrease Indent <**Ctrl Shift M**>.*

5. Indent the fifth paragraph to the second tab stop by selecting it and clicking the **Increase Indent** button twice.

6. Print a copy of the document to observe the effect of using indents.

7. Close the document <u>without</u> saving the changes that have been made.

Driving Lesson 56 - Advanced Indentation

▣ Park and Read

Right, **Left** and **First Line** indent markers are displayed on the ruler. These enable the user to produce customised indents, without the need for re-setting the tabs.

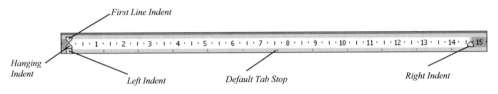

First Line Indent

Hanging Indent

Left Indent   *Default Tab Stop*   *Right Indent*

⌐ Manoeuvres

1. Open **Warehouse** again.

2. Make sure the ruler is visible. If it is not, select **View | Ruler**.

3. Position the cursor in the third paragraph.

4. Click and drag the left indent marker (square) on the left of the ruler, to **1cm** on the ruler.

5. When the mouse button is released, all lines of the paragraph will be indented to that position.

6. Click and drag the first line indent marker (top triangle) on the left of the ruler, to **2cm** on the ruler.

7. When the mouse button is released the first line of the paragraph will be indented to that position.

8. Still in the same paragraph, indent the right side of the paragraph by selecting and dragging the triangle at the bottom right of the ruler to **13cm**. When the mouse button is released the paragraph will be indented from the right.

ℹ️ *By dragging the hanging indent marker (lower triangle) to a position on the ruler, the whole paragraph will be indented, except the first line which will remain the same. Hanging indents are not part of this syllabus.*

9. Justify the paragraph. Now spend a few minutes experimenting.

10. Close **Warehouse** <u>without</u> saving.

Driving Lesson 57 - Numbering

P Park and Read

Word has the ability to automatically number lists and paragraphs. In each case, a hanging indent will also be applied. This separates the text from the numbering and improves the appearance of the document. Different styles of numbering can be applied to text, but this cannot be done using the buttons on the toolbar, you have to use the menu command.

Manoeuvres

1. Open the document **Warehouse** again.

2. Select the six paragraphs of text and number them by clicking on the **Numbering** button, 📋, on the **Formatting** toolbar.

3. Save the numbered document as **Numbers** and **preview** it.

4. Close **Print Preview**.

5. Position the cursor within the second paragraph. Click the **Numbering** button, 📋, to remove the number. Notice how *Word* has automatically renumbered the other paragraphs.

6. Remove all of the paragraph numbering by selecting the numbered paragraphs and clicking 📋.

7. Select **Format | Bullets and Numbering** and the Roman numerals from the **Numbered** tab.

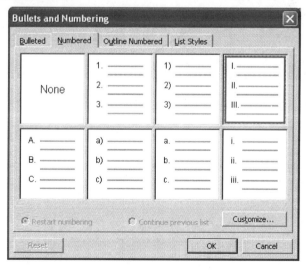

Driving Lesson 57 - Continued

The dialog box may not look exactly like the one above, but a form of Roman numerals should be available.

8. Click **Customize** and, from the **Number style** box, select the lower case numerals.

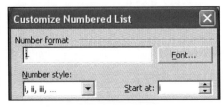

9. Now click the **Font** button and select **Trebuchet MS** (or an alternative).

10. Click **OK**, then **OK** again to apply the customised numbering.

11. Select the third item and select **Format | Bullets and Numbering**.

12. Select the **Restart numbering** option and click **OK**. The numbering now starts at **i** again.

13. Remove all of the numbering by selecting the numbered paragraphs and clicking .

14. Leave the document open for the next Driving Lesson.

Driving Lesson 58 - Bullets

Park and Read

Word has the ability to make lists and paragraphs stand out by using **Bullets**. When a bullet is applied, a hanging indent will also be applied. This separates the text and improves the appearance of the document. Different styles of bullet can be applied to text, but this cannot be done using the buttons on the toolbar, you have to use the menu command.

Manoeuvres

1.   Select all the paragraphs and click the **Bullets** button, ▦.

2.   Select the second and third paragraphs. Click the **Bullets** button again to remove the bullets.

3.   Remove all bullets from the paragraphs.

4.   Close the document, do not save the changes.

5.   Open the document **Contents**.

6.   Select all of the items on the list, then select **Format | Bullets and Numbering** and the **Bulleted** tab.

7.   Select the check (tick) bullets, as in the diagram opposite (or another bullet style if this one is not available) and click **OK**.

8.   Select the list again and display the **Bullets and Numbering** dialog box.

9.   From **Customize**, choose the **Bullet** button. Select an alternative symbol for the bullet and click **OK**, then **OK** again.

10.   Save the document as **Bulleted** and close it.

Driving Lesson 59 - Line Spacing

▣ Park and Read

Line spacing offers a simple way of improving the appearance and readability of a document. The default setting for line spacing is **Single**. Other useful line spacing settings are **Double** and 1½. However, this may not be suitable if creating a list or a table, or if a feature such as superscript is used.

⌐ Manoeuvres

1. Open the document **Camera**. Remove the top line and add your own name to the bottom of the document.

2. Select all the text, then select **Format | Paragraph**.

3. With the **Indents and Spacing** tab selected, change the **Alignment** to justified by selecting **Justified** from the drop down list.

4. Change the **Line spacing** to double by selecting **Double** from the drop down list. Click **OK** to format the text.

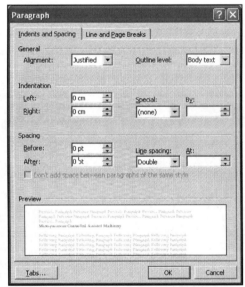

i *The **At Least, Exactly** and **Multiple** options prompt for a value in the **At** box. Enter the required value to determine the amount of space between the lines.*

5. Use the **Print Preview** facility to check the appearance of the text and then print a copy.

i *To quickly apply spacing, position the cursor within a paragraph. Press <**Ctrl 1**> for single spacing. Press <**Ctrl 2**> for double spacing.*

6. Save the document as **Cam2**. Change the line spacing for the first paragraph back to single by placing the cursor within the first paragraph and pressing <**Ctrl 1**>.

7. Print out a copy of the amended document and close it <u>without</u> saving.

Driving Lesson 60 - Spacing Between Paragraphs

P Park and Read

Spacing between paragraphs can also be adjusted. Spacing is measured in **pt**. 12pt is 1 line for a size 12 font. It's good practice to use proper paragraph spacing rather than the **<Return>** key; do it this way to make sure paragraph spacing is consistent.

☞ Manoeuvres

1.   Open the document **Warehouse**, remove the blank lines between the paragraphs and select the entire document.

2.   Select **Format | Paragraph**.

3.   To leave spacing before the paragraphs, increase the **Before** option to **24** pt.

4.   To leave spacing after the paragraphs, increase the **After** option to **12** pt.

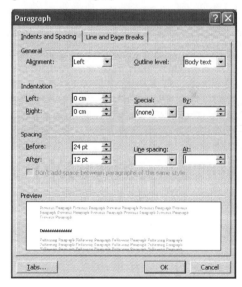

5.   Select **OK**.

i *To change the spacing before a paragraph to single line spacing, press <Ctrl 0> (zero). If the spacing is currently single line, the same key press will remove this line spacing before a paragraph.*

6.   **Preview** the document and then close <u>without</u> saving.

Driving Lesson 61 - Tab Settings

▣ Park and Read

Tabs are a precise measurement for aligning vertical rows of text in a document. Tabs are set by default every 1.27cm. New tab settings will only apply to text that has been selected, or is yet to be typed. Left alignment **Tab** settings are displayed as **L**'s on the ruler.

↱ Manoeuvres

1.   Start a new document. Select **Format | Tabs**.

2.   Set these tabs. Enter **1** cm in the **Tab stop position** box. Check the **Alignment** is **Left** and the **Leader** is **None**. Click on **Set**. Type in **10** at the **Tab stop position**. Click **Set**. Click **OK**. Notice the **L** markers on the ruler, these indicate the chosen settings.

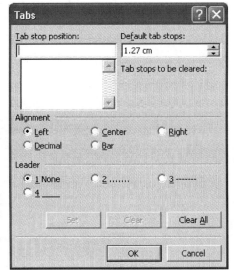

ℹ️ *Another way to set **Tabs**, is to click the required position on the ruler. An **L** will appear when it is set. Repeat to add more **Tab** stops. Change **Tab Positions** by clicking on the **L** and dragging along the ruler to the required position. Remove tabs by dragging the tab markers down, off the ruler.*

3.   Type in the following text, using the <**Tab**> key before every field to move to the next tab stop and the <**Enter**> key to start a new line. Start each new line with a <**Tab**>.

Salesperson	Sales
J Heslop	126.56
M Patel	56
K Lowe	340.75
D Green	9.5
S Evans	1200
A Hargreaves	50.98

Driving Lesson 61 - Continued

4. Save the text as **Tabs** and print a copy.

5. Select the entire document and clear the tab settings, using **Format | Tabs | Clear All | OK**.

6. With the entire document selected use the mouse and ruler to set tabs at approximately **1**cm and **7**cm.

7. Print the document and close it <u>without</u> saving changes.

8. Open the document **Contents**. Select the whole document by clicking and dragging and select **Format | Tabs** to open the **Tabs** dialog box.

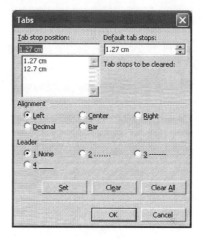

9. The two columns are too far apart. To change the tab settings, the original tabs must be cleared. Select **Clear All**.

10. Set a new tab by entering **4**cm in the **Tab stop position** box. Click **Set**.

11. Repeat this for a tab at **11**cm. Click **OK**. View the changes.

12. With the document still selected, click the left tab marker at **4**cm on the ruler and drag to about **5**cm.

13. Release the mouse button. The first column will move.

14. Click the first tab marker at **5**cm and drag it down off the ruler. The text automatically shifts to the next tab marker.

15. Create a new tab stop at **3**cm.

16. Practice using the mouse and ruler to move and remove tab markers.

17. Close **Contents** <u>without</u> saving.

Driving Lesson 62 - Tab Alignment

▣ Park and Read

Word has five types of tab settings. The important four are **Left**, **Centre**, **Right** and **Decimal**. Each of these determines how text is aligned at a particular tab stop position.

⌒ Manoeuvres

1. Re-open the document **Contents**.

2. Select the whole document and use the ruler to move the tab positions to **4cm** and **11cm**.

3. From the **Tabs** dialog box, select the **Tab stop position** at **4cm**. Notice it is left aligned.

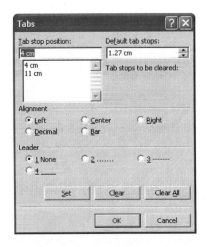

4. Click on **Right** from the **Alignment** selections. Click **Set**.

5. Repeat this procedure for the tab at **11cm**, but make it **Centre** aligned. Click **Set**.

6. Click **OK** and observe the text positioning about the tabs.

ⓘ *Tabs can be set directly from the ruler by clicking on the left end of it,* 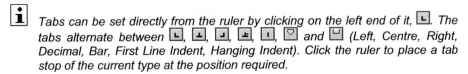 *The tabs alternate between* ⌊ ⌊ ⌊ ⌊ ⌊ ⌊ *and* ⌊ *(Left, Centre, Right, Decimal, Bar, First Line Indent, Hanging Indent). Click the ruler to place a tab stop of the current type at the position required.*

Driving Lesson 62 - Continued

7. Select the whole document again and experiment by changing the tabs into right, left and centre tabs. Close the document <u>without</u> saving.

8. Create a new document. Enter the following text, pressing **<Tab>** between each piece of text to move it to the next available tab stop. Click **Show/Hide**, [▪], to view the tab control characters (arrows pointing right) within the text. These are special, non-printing characters used by *Word* to control formatting.

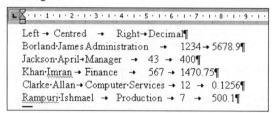

9. Select the whole document and change the current tab setting by clicking once on the ⌊ at the left end of the ruler to change it to a **Centre** tab, ⊥. Then place a centre tab at **4**cm by clicking on the number **4** on the ruler.

[i] *The tab may not be positioned exactly at 4cm. This does not matter.*

10. Click once on ⊥ to change it to a **Right** tab, ⊿ and place a right tab at **7**cm by clicking on **7** on the ruler.

11. Click once on ⊿ to change it to a **Decimal** tab, ⊥ and place a decimal tab at **9.5**cm by clicking on **9.5** on the ruler.

12. Click **Show/Hide** [▪] to hide the tab control characters. Examine the effects of the different types of tab alignment.

Left	Centred	Right	Decimal
Borland James	Administration	1234	5678.9
Jackson April	Manager	43	400
Khan Imran	Finance	567	1470.75
Clarke Allan	Computer Services	12	0.1256
Rampuri Ishmael	Production	7	500.1

13. Close the document <u>without</u> saving.

[i] *To change the type of a tab stop, you need to **remove** the **existing** one by dragging it off the ruler, before **replacing** it with one of the required type.*

Driving Lesson 63 - Adding Borders

▣ Park and Read

Borders can be created around text or whole pages. The options are: **None** - removes borders, **Box** - same border around the whole object, **Shadow** - a drop shadow around the text. **3-D** - offsets and highlights the border, while **Custom** allows borders to be applied around any side independent of the other sides. Shading can also be added to specific paragraphs for emphasis.

ℝ Manoeuvres

1. Open **Letter1**. Select all the text.

2. Select **Format | Borders and Shading**. Within the **Borders** tab there are several options: **None** allows borders to be positioned around any side independent of the other sides, **Box** will put the same border around the whole object, **Shadow** will create a drop shadow around the text. **3-D** and **Custom** allow other borders to be applied.

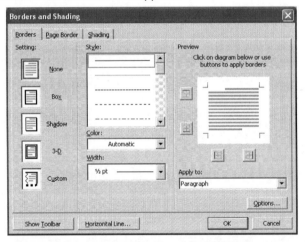

3. From the **Borders** tab select **Box**. From the **Style** options select any dashed line and then click on **OK**. A dashed line border should now surround the text of the document.

4. To remove the border, select the document first, select **Format | Borders and Shading** and from within the **Borders** tab, select **None**. Click **OK**.

ⓘ *Limited control of borders can be applied using the **Border** button,* *, found on the **Formatting Toolbar**.*

5. With the document still selected, display the **Borders and Shading** dialog box.

☞

Driving Lesson 63 - Continued

6. Click **Custom** and then click the top and bottom of the diagram at the right of the dialog box.

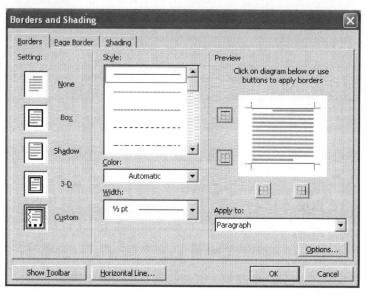

7. Click **OK**. This applies a border to the top and bottom of the text only.

8. Try giving the text a different border, by applying a different **Style**, **Color** and **Width**.

9. With the document still selected, display the **Borders and Shading** dialog box and select the **Page Border** tab.

10. Select a **Box** border with a double line style and click **OK**. Notice the difference between this **Page Border** which surrounds the whole page and the previous border which surrounds the content only.

11. Close the document <u>without</u> saving.

12. Open the document **Maneaters**.

13. To make the **Conclusion** stand out, it can be shaded. Click anywhere in the paragraph immediately under the **Conclusion** heading.

14. Select **Format | Borders and Shading** and the **Shading** tab.

15. Choose a shade of grey and click **OK** to apply the shading.

16. Print the document.

17. Close the document <u>without</u> saving.

Driving Lesson 64 - Revision

This covers the features introduced in this section. Try not to refer to the preceding Driving Lessons while completing it.

1. Open the document **Canyon**.

2. Insert the title **The Grand Canyon** on its own line at the start of the document and align it centrally.

3. Leave a blank line after the title.

4. Justify the first paragraph.

5. Right align the second paragraph.

6. Centre align the third paragraph.

7. Select the final paragraph, it is already left aligned, click the **Align Left** button and it removes left alignment and justifies the paragraph.

8. Apply left alignment using the same button.

9. Print a copy of the document in its current form.

10. Close the document <u>without</u> saving any changes.

11. Open the document **Questions**.

12. This contains 14 statements. Use a button to number them.

13. Use the **Print Preview** facility to check the results.

14. Alter the **First Line Indent** on the ruler to **2.5**cm.

15. Remove all numbering (the indent is changed).

16. Bullet this list using the button.

17. Obtain a printed copy.

18. Save a copy of the document as **Questions2**.

19. Close the document.

If you experienced any difficulty completing the Revision, refer back to the Driving Lessons in this section. Then redo the Revision.

Driving Lesson 65 - Revision

This covers the features introduced in this section. Try not to refer to the preceding Driving Lessons while completing it.

1.   Open the document **Banking**.

2.   Increase the size of the text to **18pt** and print the document.

3.   Right align the first paragraph and apply a border to it.

4.   Use justified alignment for the second paragraph.

5.   Print a copy of the document, then close it <u>without</u> saving.

6.   A printed menu must <u>be prod</u>uced for lunch. Invent a three course lunch of your choice with a small selection for each course. Separate each course with a row of suitably spaced £ signs.

7.   Add a suitable title in bold and underline.

8.   Centrally align the menu and adjust the line spacing.

9.   Print a copy of your menu, save the document as **Lunch** and close it.

10. Open the document **Books** and select all the text except for the title.

11. Apply **Numbering** to the selected lines of text.

12. Print a copy of the document.

13. Remove the **Numbering** from the lines of text and replace with **Bullets**.

14. Customise the **Bullets** by choosing alternative symbols.

15. Print a copy of the document, then close it <u>without</u> saving any changes.

16. Open **Diary**. This is a tabbed document with all the tabs set as left tabs.

17. Use the **Format | Tabs** command to change the settings for the **Time** and **Activity** columns as follows:

     Change the **Time** tab at **6.5cm** to a **Center** tab.

     Change the **Activity** tab at **11.25cm** to a **Right** tab.

18. Change the font of the headings to **Comic Sans MS**.

19. **Print Preview** the document and print it, then close the document <u>without</u> saving the changes.

If you experienced <u>any</u> difficulty completing the Revision, refer back to the Driving Lessons in this section. Then redo the Revision.

Once you are confident with the features, complete the Record of Achievement Matrix referring to the section at the end of the guide. Only when competent move on to the next Section.

Section 8
Multiple Documents

By the end of this Section you should be able to:

Switch between open Documents

Cut, Copy and Paste between Documents

Apply Headers and Footers

Apply Page Numbering

To gain an understanding of the above features, work through the **Driving Lessons** in this **Section**.

For each **Driving Lesson**, read the **Park and Read** instructions, without touching the keyboard, then work through the numbered steps of the **Manoeuvres** on the computer. Complete the **Revision Exercise(s)** at the end of the section to test your knowledge.

Driving Lesson 66 - Switch Between Documents

▣ Park and Read

Many documents can be open at the same time using *Word*. A button on the **Taskbar** represents each open document, making it easier to switch between them. The document that is being currently worked on is known as the **active document** and is distinguished from the others by having its **Taskbar** button darkly coloured (*Windows XP*) or pressed down (other *Windows* versions). If more than one document can be seen on screen, the active document is said to be present in the **active window** and is indicated by a more coloured **Title Bar**.

Opening a second document places it on screen in a new window, the document previously active can still be accessed as a button on the **Taskbar**.

⟳ Manoeuvres

1. Open the document **Retail** and type your name at the start of the document so that it can be readily identified.

2. Open the document **Camera**. The document **Retail** is minimised on the **Taskbar**.

3. Click on **Retail**'s button on the **Taskbar**.

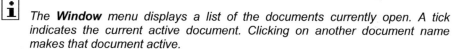

4. Open the document **Cia**. Practice switching between active documents using the **Taskbar**.

ℹ️ *The **Window** menu displays a list of the documents currently open. A tick indicates the current active document. Clicking on another document name makes that document active.*

5. Select the **Arrange All** command from the **Window** menu. All the opened documents will be shown on screen. Click on the window of **Camera** to make it active. Resize the active window to your satisfaction.

6. Click on the **Retail** window. The size of the window for **Camera** does not change.

7. Maximise **Retail** by clicking on the **Maximize** button, 🔲.

8. Select **File | Close** to close the document **Retail** in the active window. Do not save any changes made to the document.

9. Close all remaining documents, using the appropriate **Close** button, ☒ (see Driving Lesson 11), <u>without</u> saving any changes that may have been made. Maximise the *Word* screen if necessary.

Driving Lesson 67 - Cut, Copy, Paste Between Documents

▣ Park and Read

It is a relatively simple process to cut or copy text from one document and paste it into a new document, or elsewhere in the existing document. A **Smart Tag** will appear after pasting, from which **Paste Options** may be selected.

☞ Manoeuvres

1. Open the document **Parts** and select the entire document.

2. Change the font of all text to **Arial 11pt**.

3. Open the document **Planning**.

4. Select the title **Production Planning** and its associated paragraph.

5. Select the **Edit | Cut** command (or the **Cut** button, 🖾, or the key press <**Ctrl X**>).

6. Use the **Taskbar** to switch to the **Parts** document.

7. Position the cursor at the end of the document.

8. Click 🖾 or use the key press <**Ctrl V**> to paste the paragraph of text at the end of the document.

9. Click the **Smart Tag**, 🖾 , which appears after the pasted text to see the paste options.

10. Click **Match Destination Formatting** to convert the pasted text to the same format as the existing text.

11. Press <**Enter**> to separate the paragraphs as required.

12. Switch back to **Planning**.

13. Select paragraph number 7, complete with its title. Use the **Copy** and **Paste** commands to copy this to the end of the **Parts** document.

14. Adjust the spacing as necessary.

15. Try moving and/or copying text from the **Parts** document to **Planning**.

16. Close the documents <u>without</u> saving.

Driving Lesson 68 - Headers and Footers

▣ Park and Read

Headers and **Footers** are common areas at the top and/or bottom of each page. You can type text into a header or footer, so that it will appear on every page in the document. When such text is found at the top of a page it is called a **Header**; those at the bottom are termed **Footers**. Headers and Footers can be placed on alternate pages, or the same header/footer on every page.

☞ Manoeuvres

1. Open the document **Retail**. Delete the title and two blank lines at the top.

2. Check under **File | Page Setup | Layout** that neither **Different odd and even** nor **Different first page** is checked for **Headers and Footers**.

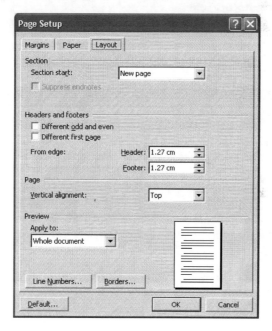

3. Click **OK**.

4. Select **View | Header and Footer**.

Driving Lesson 68 - Continued

5.   In the box provided, enter **<Tab> All About Computers <Enter> <Tab> By I. Knowitall**. This is then a two line header.

6.   Select this text, change the font colour to red and the font to **Tahoma**.

7.   Select **Switch Between Header and Footer**, 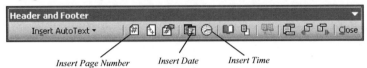, from the **Header and Footer** toolbar to switch to the **Footer**. Features such as the date, time and page numbering can be added by selecting buttons from the toolbar.

Insert Page Number   *Insert Date*   *Insert Time*

8.   To insert the name of the file and the location in which it is saved, click **Insert AutoText**.

9.   Select **Filename and path** from the drop down list.

10. Press **<Tab>** and click the **Insert Page Number** button, to place page numbering in the right corner. To close the **Footer**, click `Close`.

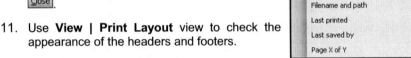

11. Use **View | Print Layout** view to check the appearance of the headers and footers.

12. **Preview** and then print a copy of the document.

i   *By selecting **File | Page Setup** (or within **Header and Footer**), the option of having different headers / footers on odd and even pages and the option of having a different first page header/footer is given.*

13. Close the document. Select **No** to lose the changes.

i   ***Headers and Footers** are not visible in **Normal** document view - to see them, use either **Print Preview** or **View | Print Layout**.*

14. Open the document **Maneaters**. View the **Header and Footer**.

15. At the top left click **Insert AutoText** and select **Page X of Y** to insert page number information.

16. Check the headers in **Print Layout View** and print the document.

17. Press **<Tab>** twice then click the **Insert Date** button, , to insert the current date at the right of the header.

18. Close the document <u>without</u> saving.

Driving Lesson 69 - Page Numbering

🅿 Park and Read

Page Numbering can be added to documents by one of two methods: firstly, as part of a **header**, or secondly using the **Insert | Page Numbers** command. Various formats can be applied to page numbers.

👉 Manoeuvres

1. Open the document **Pc**. Select **Insert | Page Numbers**.

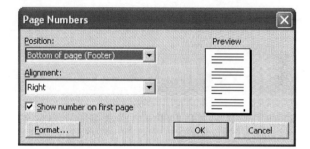

2. Click the **Format** button to view the **Page Number Format** dialog box.

3. From **Number format**, select **Upper Case Roman**.

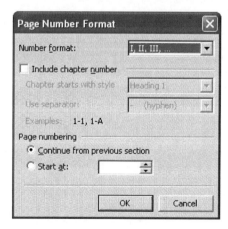

4. Click **OK** then from the **Position** box select **Top of page (Header)**.

Driving Lesson 69 - Continued

5.   From the **Alignment** box select **Left**.

6.   Make sure there is a tick in the **Show number on first page** box.

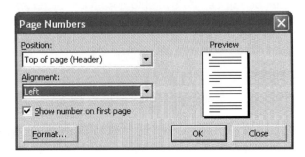

7.   Select **OK**.

8.   **Print Preview** the document - note that the **Status Bar** also shows the chosen format - **Page I, Page II**, etc. Print a copy of the document.

9.   Experiment with changing the display options within the **Page Numbers** and **Page Number Format** dialog boxes.

10.   Close the document <u>without</u> saving.

Page numbers are removed through *View | Header and Footer*. Select the *Page number* and press *<Delete>*.

Driving Lesson 70 - Revision

This covers the features introduced in this section. Try not to refer to the preceding Driving Lessons while completing it.

1. Open the document **Canyon**.

2. Centre the title and the paragraph sub headings.

3. Justify each paragraph.

4. The final paragraph, starting with **Kaibab limestone** is to be made into a list. Remove all of the commas from this paragraph.

5. After each type of rock, press <**Enter**> to create a list.

6. Add numbering to the list.

7. Add your name to the **Header** and the date to the **Footer**.

8. Print a copy of the document.

9. Close it <u>without</u> saving the changes.

10. Open the documents **Pc** and **Warehouse**.

11. Copy paragraph **5** from **Warehouse – The computer may also...**

12. Switch to the document **Pc**.

13. Paste this text at the end of the **Stock Control** paragraph on page **4**.

14. Adjust the spacing and font size as required.

15. Insert the current date in the centre of the header.

16. Enter your name at the left of the footer.

17. Apply page numbers at the right of the footer.

18. Save the document as **Multiples** and close it.

19. Close **Warehouse**.

If you experienced any difficulty completing the Revision, refer back to the Driving Lessons in this section. Then redo the Revision.

Driving Lesson 71 - Revision

This covers the features introduced in this section. Try not to refer to the preceding Driving Lessons while completing it.

1.   Open the document **News**.

2.   The news articles are to be arranged alphabetically by title. Use the menu commands **Edit | Cut** and **Edit | Paste** to rearrange the articles.

3.   Add your name to the **Footer**.

4.   Print one copy of the document.

5.   Close it <u>without</u> saving any changes.

6.   Open the document **Menu**.

7.   Centre the whole document.

8.   Increase the size of the restaurant's name, **Chez Pascale**, to **26pt**; change the font to **Lucida Handwriting**.

9.   Make it **green**.

10. Increase **Menu** to **22pt**; change the font to **Monotype Corsiva** (use an alternative font if this one is not available) and the colour to **blue**.

11. Change the size of **Entrées**, **Main Meals** and **Desserts** to **18pt** and their colour to **red**.

12. Increase the size of the meals on the menu to **14pt** and make them **blue**.

13. Add your name to the header and print a copy of the document.

14. Close it <u>without</u> saving.

If you experienced any difficulty completing the Revision, refer back to the Driving Lessons in this section. Then redo the Revision.

Once you are confident with the features, complete the Record of Achievement Matrix referring to the section at the end of the guide. Only when competent move on to the next Section.

Section 9
Tables

By the end of this Section you should be able to:

Insert Tables

Enter Text into Tables

Select Cells

Change Column Width

Insert and Delete Cells

Insert Rows and Columns

Apply Borders

To gain an understanding of the above features, work through the **Driving Lessons** in this **Section**.

For each **Driving Lesson**, read the **Park and Read** instructions, without touching the keyboard, then work through the numbered steps of the **Manoeuvres** on the computer. Complete the **Revision Exercise(s)** at the end of the section to test your knowledge.

Driving Lesson 72 - Tables

🅿 Park and Read

Word provides an easy way to create and edit organised rows and columns of tabular data (without tabs) using the table feature. This feature is also useful for creating forms such as invoices that are formatted in tabular form. Tables consist of rows, from top to bottom and columns, which run from left to right, to create cells as in spreadsheets.

👌 Manoeuvres

1. Create a new document. To create a table with **4** rows and **4** columns, move the cursor to where the table is to begin. Select **Table | Insert | Table**.

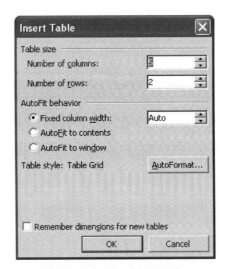

2. In the **Insert Table** dialog box, enter **4** in the **Number of columns** box and **4** in the **Number of rows** box (these numbers can be typed in or the arrowheads can be clicked to change the numbers).

3. Click **OK** to create the table. Leave the document open for the next Driving Lesson.

ℹ️ *An alternative way to create a table is to use the **Insert Table** button, ▦, from the **Standard Toolbar**. Click and drag across for the number of columns and down for the number of rows required. Once the mouse button is released, the table will be drawn.*

Driving Lesson 73 - Entering Text

Park and Read

Once a table has been created, it is simple to enter text and move around within it. Text is edited using the normal methods. It is probably easier to type the text into the table first and then return to format the table later, i.e. correct column widths, etc.

Manoeuvres

1. Use the table created in the previous Driving Lesson. Movement forwards within a table is with **<Tab>**. Use **<Shift Tab>** to move backwards (clicking in the appropriate cell will also place the cursor). When entering text do not use **<Enter>**, unless a new line is required within the same cell, e.g. as in an address.

The cursor keys can be used, but are slow when a table is full of text.

2. Make sure that **Print Layout** view is selected.

3. Move to the first cell and enter the following text into the table. Pay no attention to how the table looks, it will be improved later.

Company	Share Price	Sector	Type of Business
Global	1240	Chemicals	Petro Chemicals
Biro Bank	300	Banking	Corporate Finance
Gibsons	130	Stores	Electrical Retailer

*As text is entered, the **Move**,⊞ and **Adjust**, □, cursors appear above and below the table in **Print Layout** view. **Move** is clicked and dragged to move the table around the page and **Adjust** is clicked and dragged to proportionately increase or decrease the size of the table.*

4. The share price for **Gibsons** has risen by 50 points. To edit the table, double click on the **130** price.

5. The number is highlighted. Type in **180** to replace the original number.

6. Save the document as **Table** and close it.

Driving Lesson 74 - Selecting Cells

P Park and Read

To act on a group of cells they must first be selected. To select a cell, or group of cells use the selection arrow. This is shown when the cursor is placed near a left cell edge of a row (white) or the top of a column (black).

Manoeuvres

1. In a new document, create a table **5** columns by **5** rows.

2. Select the first cell by moving near to its left edge and clicking the left mouse button when the arrow is displayed, as in the diagram.

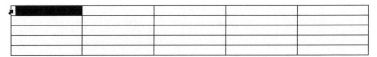

3. Move the mouse down and click again to remove the selection. Select the second column by moving near to the top edge of the column and clicking the mouse when the selection arrow is displayed.

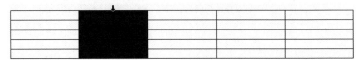

4. Select the entire third row by double clicking when the arrow is displayed at the edge of any cell in the row or by clicking once when the arrow is in the selection bar on the left.

5. Select the nine cells in the middle of the table by clicking and dragging.

6. Click anywhere in the table and select **Table | Select Table**. The whole table is selected.

7. Close the document <u>without</u> saving.

i *Rows and columns can also be selected by placing the cursor within the row/column then using **Table | Select Row/Column**.*

Driving Lesson 75 - Changing the Column Width/Row Height

P Park and Read

The most important advantage of the tables feature over the tab stops is the ability to change the width of the column interactively. Note that the total width of the table is restricted by the space available between the margins. Reduce the width of small columns before widening others.

Manoeuvres

1.   Open the document **Table**, created in Driving Lesson ~~82~~ *72* and saved in Driving Lesson ~~83~~. *73*

2.   Select **View | Ruler** to display the ruler, if it is not already on the screen.

3.   Move the cursor into the table. When inside the table, the ruler shows the table column divides as symbols within the ruler.

4.   A column width can be changed by clicking on the divide, then dragging to a new position before releasing the mouse button. A double-headed arrow appears when the mouse pointer is over the division.

5.   Reduce the first three columns (make **Share Price** fit on two lines).

6.   Now select **Table | Select | Table**, then **Table | Table Properties**. Select the **Row** tab, check **Specify height** and enter **1 cm** in the box. Click **OK**.

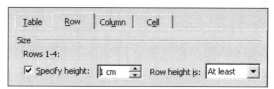

i *Column width, cell size and text alignment can be changed from the **Column** and **Cell** tabs.*

7.   Save the document as **Table1**.

8.   Print a copy of the document and leave open for the next Driving Lesson.

i *Row Heights can also be changed using the ruler. Switch to **Print Layout** and use the **Vertical Ruler**. Hold <Alt> whilst changing the row height to view the correct measurements on the ruler.*

Driving Lesson 76 - Inserting & Deleting Rows & Columns

▣ Park and Read

It is possible to change the size of a table by adding or deleting rows and columns. Rows and columns can be added to or removed from the edges or the inside of the table.

⌕ Manoeuvres

1. Using the document **Table1**, place the cursor anywhere in the first column, select **Table | Insert | Columns to the Left** to insert one new column at the left edge of the table.

> ⓘ *An alternative method of inserting rows and columns is to select **Table | Insert Cells** and select **Insert entire row** or **Insert entire column**, then click **OK**. To add more rows into a table place the cursor in the last cell of the table and press <Tab>. New rows are added accordingly.*

2. With the column selected, use the number button, ▤, to number the rows of text.

3. Make the column as small as possible, but ensure the numbers can be seen.

4. Widen the second column, using the symbols on the ruler. Place the cursor in the numbered row 2, and insert a new row by selecting **Table | Insert | Rows Above**. The rows are automatically renumbered.

> ⓘ *The **Table** button on the **Standard Toolbar** changes depending on what is selected in the table. For example, selecting a row will change the button to **Insert Rows**, ▤.*

5. To delete the new row, select the row, then **Table | Delete | Rows**.

6. Select the **Sector** column and insert a new column to the left.

7. Now delete this column. Make sure it is selected, then select **Table | Delete Columns**.

8. Save the document with the same name and leave it open.

> ⓘ *Multiple cells that are next to each other in a row or column can be merged into a single cell by selecting them and then selecting **Table | Merge Cells**.*

Driving Lesson 77 - Table Borders/Shading

▣ Park and Read

The default border and lines applied to tables can be changed. Various types of lines, borders and shading can be added to an entire table, or to selected cells, rows or columns. There are also a number of predefined styles available.

☞ Manoeuvres

1. Use the document **Table1**. Move to the second row and select the whole row. Change the border to double by selecting **Format | Borders and Shading**. With the **Borders** tab displayed, make sure **All** is selected from **Setting**, select a double line from the **Style** and click **OK**.

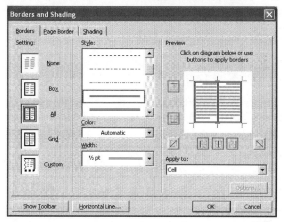

2. Select the whole table and remove the lines by choosing **None** from **Setting**. Click **OK**.

3. Even with the borders removed there may still be faint lines, called **gridlines**, defining the table. If they are not shown select **Table | Show Gridlines**. These lines are for guidance only when working on the table, they do not print. To remove them from the screen, select **Table | Hide Gridlines**.

4. Select a range of cells within the table and continue to experiment with different **Styles**. Try changing the **Color** and **Width**.

ℹ️ *Alternatively, click the **Borders** button,* ▦ ▾*, from the **Formatting Toolbar** and select an option from the list.*

5. Select the first row. In the **Borders and Shading** dialog box select the **Shading** tab. Click on various squares within the **Fill** palette and observe the effects in the **Preview** panel. Select a **Fill** option and click **OK** to apply your chosen background colour to the cells.

6. Save the document using the same name and close it.

Driving Lesson 78 - Revision

This covers the features introduced in this section. Try not to refer to the preceding Driving Lessons while completing it.

1.   Start a new document.

2.   Create a table with **3** columns and **11** rows.

3.   Enter the following headings in the columns: **Author**, **Title** and **Type**.

4.   Open the document **Books**.

5.   Print a copy of the document, so that you can copy the information, then close it.

6.   Enter the information from **Books** into the table.

7.   Make all the headings bold.

8.   Shade the background of the headings with **Yellow** and shade the rest of the cells with **Teal**.

9.   Change the font of the headings to **Tahoma** (use an alternative font if this one is not available) and change the **Font Color** to **White**.

10. Centre all of the text and change the colour of the remaining text to **Bright Green**.

11. Save the table as **My Table** and close it.

i   *Check the answers at the back of the guide for an indication of how your document should look.*

If you experienced any difficulty completing the Revision, refer back to the Driving Lessons in this section. Then redo the Revision.

Driving Lesson 79 - Revision

This covers the features introduced in this section. Try not to refer to the preceding Driving Lessons while completing it.

1. Start a new document.

2. Create a new table to match the table below, an invoice. You will need to consult the final [i] in **Driving Lesson 76**.

Invoice				
Ref No	Description	Qty	Price	Total
Subtotal				
VAT				
Total				

3. Save the document as **Invoice** and close it.

4. Start a new document.

5. Create the following table with the text, lines and shading:

Date	Order Form	Terms	
Title	Type	Licence Number	Price
Total			

6. Save the document as **Order Form**.

7. Print a copy of the table.

8. To allow room for more orders, insert three new rows above the bottom row.

9. Save the changes and then close the document.

If you experienced any difficulty completing the Revision, refer back to the Driving Lessons in this section. Then redo the Revision.

Once you are confident with the features, complete the Record of Achievement Matrix referring to the section at the end of the guide. Only when competent move on to the next Section.

Section 10
Document Manipulation

By the end of this Section you should be able to:

Select Paper Size

Change Page Orientation

Change Margins

Insert Page Breaks

Apply Styles

To gain an understanding of the above features, work through the **Driving Lessons** in this **Section**.

For each **Driving Lesson**, read the **Park and Read** instructions, without touching the keyboard, then work through the numbered steps of the **Manoeuvres** on the computer. Complete the **Revision Exercise(s)** at the end of the section to test your knowledge.

Driving Lesson 80 - Document Setup

🅿 Park and Read

The default paper size used by *Word* is **A4** but, because some situations call for the use of non-standard paper sizes, this can be changed. The size selected will depend upon both the printer and the particular application in use. Page

Orientation can also be changed – a document can be printed in **Portrait** or **Landscape**.

Margins determine the distance between the text and the edges of the paper. The top and bottom margins are used for features such as headers, footers and page numbering. A large top margin can be set when working with headed notepaper. The top and bottom margins are, by default, set to 2.54cm.

Side margins can be changed to allow space for binding (**Gutter margin**), to change the length of the document and to improve its readability. By default, the side margins (left and right) are set at 3.17cm. *Word* has many predefined settings for page size and margins available.

☞ Manoeuvres

1. Open the document **Retail**. Move to the very beginning of the document. Create a space and type the words **Page Size 23cm x 18cm**.

2. Select **File | Page Setup** and the **Paper** tab.

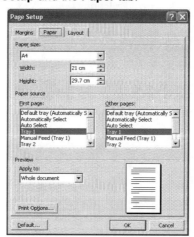

3. Change the width to **18**cm and the height to **23**cm, either by editing the numbers or by using the up and down arrows. Note that the **Paper Size** box has changed to **Custom Size**. Click **OK**.

Driving Lesson 80 - Continued

4.   Preview the document. Print out the first page only.

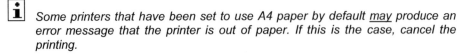 *Some printers that have been set to use A4 paper by default <u>may</u> produce an error message that the printer is out of paper. If this is the case, cancel the printing.*

5.   To return the paper size back to **A4**, select **File | Page Setup | Paper** tab, click the drop down arrow of the **Paper size** box and select **A4**. Click **OK**.

6.   To change the **Orientation** of the document to **Landscape**, select **File | Page Setup | Margins**.

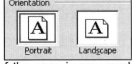

7.   From **Orientation**, select **Landscape**, then click **OK**. Notice the **Ruler** bar across the top of the page is now much longer.

8.   Print page **1** only, to see the effect and compare it with the earlier printed copy.

9.   Close the document <u>without</u> saving the changes.

10.   Open the document **Scents**.

11.   To change the document margins, select **File | Page Setup | Margins**.

12.   Increase the **Top**, **Bottom**, **Left** and **Right** margins to **5cm**, either by editing the numbers or by using the up and down arrows.

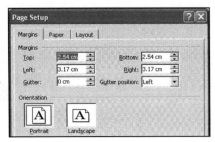

13.   Click **OK**.

14.   Justify the text and select **View | Print Layout** to see the effects of the margin settings.

15.   Print the document and close it <u>without</u> saving.

Driving Lesson 81 - Page Breaks

▣ Park and Read

It may be necessary to start a new page by choice. This is known as forcing a new page. Don't repeatedly use the **<Enter>** key to create a new page; it's good practice to insert a **page break**. When a page break is inserted in **Normal** view, a dotted line appears in the text, where the break has been inserted. If this is done in **Print Layout** view, a new page appears on the screen.

⟦⟧ Manoeuvres

1. Open the document **Packages**.

2. Divide the document into three pages by forcing new pages after the first and third paragraphs. Position the cursor in the blank line after the paragraph and then select **Insert | Break**, then **Page break** and click **OK**. Alternatively, to avoid including the blank lines on the new page, position the cursor at the start of the next paragraph.

 Pressing <Ctrl Enter> also inserts a page break.

3. Move the insertion point into the second paragraph. Check that **Page 2** appears in the **Status Bar**.

4. Select the **Print Preview** button to see the resulting three pages. If there is only one page on screen, move to the **Multiple Pages** button, click and drag across until it reads **1 x 3 Pages**. Release the mouse button.

5. Select the multiple pages button and set it to **1 x 2 Pages**.

6. Close the **Print Preview** feature to return to the document.

7. To remove a page break in **Normal View**, click on it and press **<Delete>**. Remove the page breaks to restore the document to a single page.

8. Check that you have a one page document by looking at the **Status Bar**, then close the document <u>without</u> saving.

Driving Lesson 82 - Styles

▣ Park and Read

Styles are pre-created formats consisting of paragraph and font formats. When they are applied, text will be formatted accordingly. Styles also ensure that formatting is consistent throughout a document.

⌐ Manoeuvres

1. Open the document **Retail**.

2. Highlight the first heading, **Computers and Retailing**.

3. Select **Format | Styles and Formatting** to display the **Styles and Formatting Task Pane**.

4. Ensure **All Styles** is selected from the **Show** box at the bottom of the pane.

5. Scroll through the **Styles** list and position the pointer over **Heading 1**. Read the description that appears as a **ToolTip**.

6. Click on **Heading 1**. The formatting associated with this style is applied to the selected text

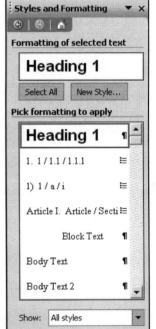

> **COMPUTERS AND RETAILING**

ℹ *Styles can also be selected from the **Style** box found on the **Formatting Toolbar**,* 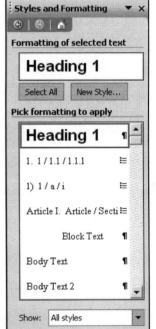 Heading 1 ▼

7. Scroll through the document and highlight the heading **1. Item Identification**. Select the style **Heading 2** from the **Task Pane** and apply **it** to the text.

> *1. Item Identification*

8. Scroll through the document, formatting all numbered headings as **Heading 2** and all lettered headings, e.g. **A) Bar-Coding**, as **Heading 3**.

☞

Driving Lesson 82 - Continued

9. A style can be applied to a paragraph of text. Place the cursor anywhere in the first paragraph.

10. Choose the **Block Text** style from the **Task Pane** list. Notice how the whole paragraph has the style applied.

COMPUTERS AND RETAILING

Computers can assist in many of the functions of a retailing organisation. Among areas which can be assisted by computers are:

1) Item Identification and Customer receipts.

---

11. Scroll down the document until the **1. Item Identification** heading is displayed.

12. Double click the word **traditional** to select it. This ensures the style will only be applied to the word rather than the paragraph.

13. Select the **Emphasis** style to apply the style to the selected word only.

---

1. Item Identification

The *traditional* price ticket on items has been replaced by a variety of new methods which can assist retailers by providing easy input of sales information.

---

14. Print the document, then save it as **Styles** and close it.

15. Close the **Task Pane**.

Driving Lesson 83 - Revision

This covers the features introduced in this section. Try not to refer to the preceding Driving Lessons while completing it.

1.   Open the document **Pc**.

2.   Switch to **Print Layout View** and notice the number of pages the document contains.

3.   Change the paper size to **Legal 8½ x 14 in**.

4.   What happens to the number of pages?

5.   Move to page **3** and insert a page break after the **Modems and Networks** paragraph, so that **Computer Applications** starts page **4**.

6.   Print the last two pages of the document and close it <u>without</u> saving.

7.   Open the document **Paper**.

8.   Change the left and right margins to **5cm** and change the page orientation to **Landscape**.

9.   Change all of the bold headings to **Heading 1**.

10. Change the first sentence after each heading to **Heading 2**.

11. Print preview the document.

12. Print the document and close it <u>without</u> saving.

13. Open the document **Headlines**.

14. Apply the style **Headliner** to all headings in the document.

15. Apply the style **Information** to the rest of the text.

16. Print the document.

17. Close the document <u>without</u> saving.

18. Close the **Task Pane** if it is still open.

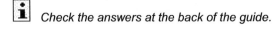 *Check the answers at the back of the guide.*

If you experienced any difficulty completing the Revision, refer back to the Driving Lessons in this section. Then redo the Revision.

Once you are confident with the features, complete the Record of Achievement Matrix referring to the section at the end of the guide. Only when competent move on to the next Section.

Section 11 Mail Merge

By the end of this Section you should be able to:

Create a Main Document

Create a Data Source

Edit the Main Document

Perform Mail Merge

To gain an understanding of the above features, work through the **Driving Lessons** in this **Section**.

For each **Driving Lesson**, read the **Park and Read** instructions, without touching the keyboard, then work through the numbered steps of the **Manoeuvres** on the computer. Complete the **Revision Exercise(s)** at the end of the section to test your knowledge.

Driving Lesson 84 - Mail Merge

▣ Park and Read

The **Merge** feature is used to combine a **Main Document** (a letter, for example), with a separate list - the **Data Source** (names and addresses, for example), into one document. These two files, when merged, create a personalised copy of the document for everyone on the list. Mailing labels to the same group of people can be created, if required, using the same technique.

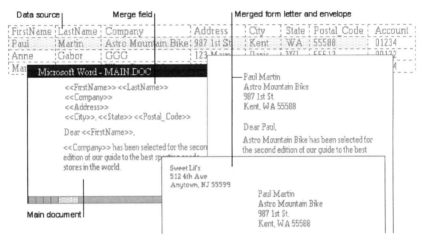

Two important terms that are used with merging are **Field** and **Record**. The following example shows **fields** (columns - Surname, First name, Street, Town, County) and **records** (rows - information for each person):

Surname	First name	Street	Town	County
Chapman	Ian	7 The Avenue	Boldon	Tyne & Wear
Peagram	Norma	5 St Georges	Morpeth	Northumberland

A **Data Source** is a document containing all the records used in a merged document in table format. These documents need a great deal of planning as they can be used for various applications.

It is best to break the information into as many fields as possible. For example, **Name** could be a field, but, **Surname**, **First Name** and **Initial** would be more useful, depending on requirements. **Paul French** entered in one field cannot be used in a merged document as **P French**, **Paul**, **Mr French** or **Mr P French**. Every record must have exactly the same number of fields, so some fields may have to be left blank.

Data Source files are used many times. As situations change, it will be necessary to add new records, change records and delete records. These changes can be made using the standard editing techniques.

Driving Lesson 85 - Creating the Main Document

Park and Read

The first step in mail merging is to create the **Main Document** to form the basis for the merge. A main document can take a range of formats, such as form letters, mailing labels, envelopes or catalogues. *Word* gives a great deal of assistance in the form of the **Mail Merge Wizard**. This comprises six steps that define the complete **Mail Merge** process. You can move back and forth through the steps by using the **Next** and **Previous** links.

Manoeuvres

1. Create a new document, and select **Tools | Letters and Mailings | Mail Merge**. The **Mail Merge Task Pane** appears.

2. Make sure **Letters** is selected from the **Select document type** list.

3. Click ⇨ Next: Starting document to move onto step 2.

4. At step 2 choose to **Use the current document**.

Driving Lesson 85 - Continued

5.   The main document can now be created. On the first line of the blank document, enter the current date, using **Insert | Date and Time**.

6.   From the **Available formats**, select the date in the format **30 September 2002**.

7.   Add 2 blank lines. Type the following paragraph.

> **Dear**
>
> **This is just a brief reminder that the next annual conference of the Word Users' Club is only a few weeks away. Delegates are limited to 1500 this year, so please hurry and reserve your place!**
>
> **Sincerely**
>
> **Ms M S Word**

8.   Save the document with the name **Main**.

| i |

The writing of the main document can be left until step 4 if required.

9.   Click | ➡ Next: Select recipients | to move onto step 3.

10.   Leave the document open.

Driving Lesson 86 - Creating a Data Source

▣ Park and Read

An **Address List (Data Source)** can be used with any number of **Main Documents**, so its creation must be well thought out. It can be created before or after the main document and can be accessed at any time once created.

⌐ℝ Manoeuvres

1. There is an option here to use an existing list but for now select **Type a new list** then click 🔲 Create... .

2. Click **Customize** to edit the field names. At the dialog box, remove field names so that only **Title**, **Last Name**, **Company Name**, **Address Line 1**, **Address Line 2** and **City** remain. Do this by clicking on each field name that is not needed and then **Delete**, selecting **Yes** at the prompt.

3. Click **Add** to add a new field. Type **Initial** into the box provided and click **OK**. Move it to the appropriate place in the list using the **Move Up** / **Move Down** buttons. The field list is complete, click on **OK**.

4. Using the <**Tab**> key to move from field to field, enter your own details and those of **3** other people (fictional if necessary). Select **New Entry** after each record. Click **Close** to end.

5. When the **Save Address List** dialog box appears, save it to the **3 Word Processing** folder (or another folder if applicable), with the **File name** of **Data**. The data is saved as a **Microsoft Office Address List** file (*.mdb).

6. The **Mail Merge Recipients** dialog box appears. The data source can be edited here at any time. Click **OK** to close it without making any changes.

> ⓘ The **Mail Merge Recipients** button, 🖫, on the **Mail Merge Toolbar** or **Task Pane** will display that dialog box at any time.

7. Click ➪ Next: Write your letter to move on to step 4.

Driving Lesson 87 - Editing the Main Document

▣ Park and Read

After the fields have been decided, they can be incorporated into the **Main Document**.

⟲ Manoeuvres

1.   Add **2** blank lines at the top of the main document.

2.   Place the cursor at the top of the document and click [📃 More items...].

3.   Select **Title** from the drop down list and click **Insert**. Click **Close**.

4.   Add a space in the document after the **Title** field, then select the **Insert Merge Fields** button, 📃 from the **Mail Merge** toolbar. This time select **Initial** and click **Insert**. Complete the fields as below (Remember to add spaces where necessary or press <**Enter**> to move to the next line).

> <<Title>> <<Initial>> <<Last Name>>
> <<Company Name>>
> <<Address Line 1>>
> <<Address Line 2>>
> <<City>>

ⓘ *Adding a standard address block like the one above can be made easier by using the **Insert Address Block** button,* 📃 *, from the toolbar or the **Task Pane**.*

5.   After **Dear** in the main part of the document, insert a space then the **Title** field followed by another space and then **Last Name**.

6.   Save the document under the same name, **Main** and leave it open.

Driving Lesson 88 - Merging

🅿 Park and Read

The hardest part of mail merge is the creation of the main and data source documents. It is easy to merge the two files. After the merge, you can print the merged letters. You can also save them as a separate file, if you want to use them again.

Manoeuvres

1. Click ⇨ Next: Preview your letters on the **Task Pane** to move to step **5** where the merged letters can be previewed and printed.

2. Use the **Next Recipient** button, >> , to move through the final letters.

ℹ️ *There are options here to amend the recipients list (the data source) or to individually exclude any particular letter from the merge.*

3. Click ⇨ Next: Complete the merge to complete the merge.

4. Read the information in the **Task Pane** then click 🖨 Print... to select letters for printing.

5. Make sure **All** is selected from the **Merge to Printer** dialog box and click **OK**.

6. Click **OK** from the **Print** dialog box to print the merged file.

7. To save the merged file, click 📄 Edit individual letters... in the **Task Pane**.

8. In the **Merge to New Document** dialog box, select **All** and click **OK**.

9. Save the file as **Merge** and close all documents, saving any changes if prompted.

Driving Lesson 89 - Open a Data Source

P Park and Read

You don't always have to create a data source from scratch. Existing data source files can be used when performing mail merge.

Manoeuvres

1. Open the document **Main** (click **Yes** at the prompt), select **Tools | Letters and Mailings | Mail Merge** to display the **Mail Merge Task Pane**.

2. Because this is already a main document the **Mail Merge** should start at step **3, Select recipients**. Select the option to **Use an existing list** and click 🔲 Select a different list...

3. In the **Select Data Source** dialog box make sure **Look in** shows the location of the data files. Select **Clients** from the list of files and click **Open**.

4. Because this main document has already been used with a different data source, it still contains the merge fields relating to that source. These may not apply to the new data and they can either be removed or replaced with one of the new fields.

5. Click **Remove Field** for the first field, **Title** and the next one, **Initial**. For the next field, **Last Name**, select **Name** from the drop down list of new fields and click **OK**. This will replace the old field with the new one.

6. For the remainder of the fields, replace **Company Name** with **Company**, **Address Line 1** with **Street**, **Address Line 2** with **Town** and remove **City**.

7. Click **OK** at the **Mail Merge Recipients** list, then continue through the remaining **Mail Merge** steps as before. Close all documents <u>without</u> saving.

8. The mail merge feature also makes it easy to create labels for your mass mailing. Start a new document and display the **Mail Merge Task Pane** and the **Mail Merge** toolbar. To create mailing labels, select **Labels** at step **1**. At step 2 click **Label options** to select the required format.

9. At step 3 select **Use an existing list** and click **Browse** to find **Client** from the supplied data files. Click **Open** then **OK** to accept the **Recipient** list.

10. At step 4 **Insert** all available fields onto the first label, then in the **Task Pane** click **Update all labels** to copy the layout to the other labels on the page (don't worry if extra fields appear at this stage; they will disappear at step **5**).

11. Review the labels at step 5 then complete the merge.

12. Print page **1** of the labels only, then close all documents <u>without</u> saving.

Driving Lesson 90 - Revision

This covers the features introduced in this section. Try not to refer to the preceding Driving Lessons while completing it.

1. Create a short letter, which is to be the main document, informing a company of a visit, using the following text:

   Dear

   Just to confirm our visit to your company on   regarding a health and safety inspection.

   Yours sincerely

   Janet Orr

   Cleaning Inspector

2. Save the main document as **Main Letter**.

3. Create a data source file with **4** records containing the field names **Title**, **Last Name**, **Company Name**, **Address Line 1**, **City** and **Date**.

4. Save this as **Data Source**.

5. Insert the merge field names in the appropriate places in the main document.

6. Merge the two files and print a copy of the four letters, saving the merged document as **Merged2**.

7. Close the merged document.

8. Open the document **Buslet**; this is a prepared mail merge letter. Click **Yes** at the prompt to continue.

9. If prompted, locate the data source as **Clients** from the data files.

10. Use the **Mail Merge Recipients** button to view the data attached.

11. Click on **OK** to return to the **Main Document**.

12. Use the **Mail Merge Task Pane** to merge to a new document and prepare the letters. Preview the letters.

13. Close all documents <u>without</u> saving.

If you experienced any difficulty completing the Revision, refer back to the Driving Lessons in this section. Then redo the Revision.

Driving Lesson 91 - Revision

This covers the features introduced in this section. Try not to refer to the preceding Driving Lessons while completing it.

1. Start a new document and create a mail merge **Letter** from the **current document**.

2. Edit the main document by inserting the date (first format) and typing the following letter:

    Dear

    I am planning a party for the ghosts of great naval explorers, to be held on board my ship, the Mary Rose, in the Solent. Please arrive in your own vessel, the   and a rowing boat will transfer you to the party. I look forward to seeing through you.

    Sincerely

    Henry VIII

3. Save the main document as **Explorers**.

4. Create a data source document containing these fields: **First Name**, **Last Name**, **Country** and **Vessel**.

5. Save this document as **Shipping List** and add the following records:

Christopher	**Columbus**	**Spain**	**Santa Maria**
Francis	**Drake**	**England**	**Golden Hind**
James	**Cook**	**England**	**Endeavour**

6. Add these fields to the top of the main document:

    <<First Name>> <<Last Name>>
    <<Country>>

7. After **Dear** add **<<First Name>>** and after **your own vessel, the** add **<<Vessel>>**.

8. Remove any surplus space if necessary.

9. Save the document under the same name.

10. Merge to a new document, add your name to the header and print the document.

11. Close all documents, saving, if prompted.

If you experienced any difficulty completing the Revision, refer back to the Driving Lessons in this section. Then redo the Revision.

Once you are confident with the features, complete the Record of Achievement Matrix referring to the section at the end of the guide. Only when competent move on to the next Section.

Section 12
Objects

By the end of this Section you should be able to:

Insert a Picture

Insert an Image from File

Insert Charts

Move and Resize a Picture, Image or Chart

To gain an understanding of the above features, work through the **Driving Lessons** in this **Section**.

For each **Driving Lesson**, read the **Park and Read** instructions, without touching the keyboard, then work through the numbered steps of the **Manoeuvres** on the computer. Complete the **Revision Exercise(s)** at the end of the section to test your knowledge.

Driving Lesson 92 - Inserting a Picture

🅿 Park and Read

Any picture or graphic stored on the computer or available online can be placed at the insertion point on a document. *Word* is supplied with many pictures in the **Clipart** folder. Other graphics, from other programs can also be incorporated into documents - providing they are in a format that *Word* can import.

☞ Manoeuvres

1. Open the document **Cat** and click in the blank line at the end of the text.

2. Select **Insert | Picture | Clip Art**.

> ℹ️ *As mentioned in an earlier exercise Office 2003 allows ClipArt to be downloaded from the Microsoft web site directly into Word.*

> ℹ️ *If the **Add ClipArt to Organizer** dialog box appears, click on **Now** then **OK**.*

3. In the **Clip Art Task Pane**, type **animals** in the **Search for** box and click **Go**.

4. A number of relevant images will be displayed in the **Task Pane**, (there may be a slight delay as they load). Select the clip at the right (or an alternative if this is not available) by clicking on it. It will be inserted into the document.

5. Select the picture in the document by clicking on it. Handles (squares) will appear around the image to indicate it is selected and the **Picture** toolbar will be displayed.

Driving Lesson 92 - Continued

6.   With the picture still selected, press <**Delete**> to remove it.

7.   There should be a large selection of pictures in clipart. Click the **Organize clips** link at the bottom of the **Task Pane**.

8.   The **Microsoft Clip Organizer** dialog box is displayed. Click the **+** to the left of **Office Collections** to reveal the available categories.

9.   Click on any **Category** to display the associated clips.

> **i** *To insert an image from the **Organizer**, **Copy** and **Paste** must be used.*

10.   Spend some time viewing pictures from the various categories then close the **Organizer** dialog box.

> **i** *A star ▨, at the bottom right of a clip indicates it is an animated clip.*

11.   Close the **Clip Art Task Pane**, using its **Close** button, ☒ .

12.   To insert an image from file, click after the end of the text again and select **Insert | Picture | From File**.

13.   In the **Insert Picture** dialog box, make sure **Look in** shows the location of the supplied data files and select the **cat** file.

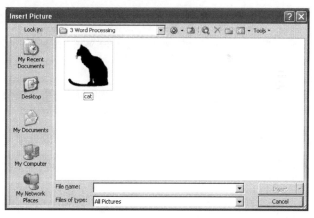

> **i** *This dialog box can be displayed with different views. The one shown here is **Preview** view.*

14.   Click **Insert**. The image is inserted in the document.

15.   To select the image and display the handles, click on it.

16.   Delete the cat image by pressing <**Delete**> then close the document without saving.

Driving Lesson 93 - Inserting Charts

Park and Read

A chart can be added to a document to display information professionally. This could be useful when producing a report containing figures, because sometimes a visual representation of figures can help make them easier to understand. Other objects such as images, pictures and drawn objects can be inserted in a similar way.

Manoeuvres

1.   Start a new document. From the menu select **Insert | Picture** then **Chart**.

2.   After a few seconds a chart will appear in the background with the datasheet visible.

▦ Document5 - Datasheet			A	B	C	D	E
			1st Qtr	2nd Qtr	3rd Qtr	4th Qtr	
1	▥	East	20.4	27.4	90	20.4	
2	▥	West	30.6	38.6	34.6	31.6	
3	▥	North	45.9	46.9	45	43.9	

3.   In the datasheet, position the mouse over **1st Qtr** and click. Type in **Jan**. Press <**Tab**> to move to the next column and enter **Feb**. Enter **Mar** and **Apr** in the next two columns.

4.   Using the above process enter the following information:

	Jan	Feb	Mar	Apr
Word	200	150	175	190
Access	300	250	300	50
Excel	220	150	100	275

5.   Click the **View Datasheet** button, ▦, to remove the datasheet and view the graph.

6.   Click on the document away from the chart to insert it into the document.

7.   Save the document as **Objects** and leave it open for the next Driving Lesson.

i   *To edit the chart, double click on it from the document. If necessary, click the* **View Datasheet** *button,* ▦*, to display and edit the datasheet.*

Driving Lesson 94 - Move and Resize Objects

P Park and Read

It is a simple process to move pictures and any other objects around, just click and drag! Resizing is slightly more difficult. After the object is selected, handles are displayed (small squares in the corners and on the sides). By clicking and dragging a handle it is possible to make the object larger or smaller.

Manoeuvres

1. Use the document **Objects** created in the previous Driving Lesson. To resize the chart, first click on it once and notice the squares (handles) around the outline of the picture. The picture is now selected.

2. Select the bottom right handle of the chart and increase its size using the handle to click and drag down and to the right.

Dragging the corner handles of an object changes its size but keeps its relative dimensions the same, i.e. a square will still be square. Dragging the middle handles of an object will deform the shape, i.e. stretch or squash it.

3. To make it possible to move an object, its text wrapping properties must be amended. Right click on the chart and select **Format Object**.

4. From the **Layout** tab select a **Square** wrapping style and click **OK**. The handles should now be white. Move the mouse over the chart. The cursor changes to ↔ when it is in a position to move the chart.

5. Click and drag the chart to a different position on the page and click away from it to deselect it.

6. In the same document, use **Insert | Picture | Clip Art**, search for **cars**, and insert a suitable clip on to the page.

7. Click to select the new picture (it may be partially obscured by the chart). Click the **Text Wrapping** button from the **Picture** toolbar and select **Square**.

Driving Lesson 94 - Continued

8.   Click and drag the picture (not the handles) to another position further down the document.

9.   Make sure the picture still has handles, i.e. it is selected. Move the pointer over one of the handles (the mouse pointer changes). Click and drag inwards to make the picture smaller or outwards to make it larger.

10. Demonstrate the difference between resizing with the corner handles and with the middle handles.

11. Finally make the image about half its original size and position it well away from the chart.

12. Insert the image **Cat** from the data files. To be able to move the image, right click on it and select **Format Picture**.

13. Select the **Layout** tab and click **Square**, then **OK**. The handles of the image change from black to white, showing that it can be dragged about the page.

14. Click and drag the cat to the top right corner of the page. If the cat obscures the chart, move the chart out of the way.

15. Use a corner handle to resize it, making it half its original size.

16. Drawn objects can also be added to a document. Select **View | Toolbars** and make sure **Drawing** is selected.

17. Click the **Rectangle** tool from the **Drawing** toolbar. If a blank drawing placeholder appears, press **<Esc>** to remove it. Click and drag with the drawing tool cursor to create a rectangle.

18. A drawn object is 'movable' by default, and can be moved and resized in the same way as an image object. Click and drag a corner handle to resize it, click and drag in the centre to move it.

i *Ovals, Lines and a range of AutoShapes can be added in the same way.*

19. Save **Objects** using the same name, leave the document open.

Driving Lesson 95 - Copy and Paste Objects

⊞ Park and Read

Objects such as images and charts can be copied to a different location within a document or to a different document. <u>When an object is copied the original is unchanged</u>.

⟰ Manoeuvres

1.   Using the document **Objects**, select the chart.

2.   Click the **Copy** button, 🖻, the menu selection **Edit | Copy** or the key press <**Ctrl C**> to copy the object

3.   Click **Paste**, 🖻, or select **Edit | Paste** or use the key press <**Ctrl V**> to paste a copy of the original on top of the first chart.

4.   Make the copy about half its original size and drag it to a blank area of the page.

5.   Select the original chart.

6.   Press <**Delete**> to delete it.

ⓘ *Pictures and images are deleted in the same way.*

7.   Copy the picture of the car.

8.   Paste a copy of the picture into the current document.

9.   Start a new document and paste the car picture into it.

10.   Insert the **cat** image from the data files into the new document.

11.   Copy the cat and then click away from it to deselect it.

12.   Paste the cat into the same document.

13.   Use the **Taskbar** to move to **Objects**.

14.   Paste the cat image into this document.

15.   Copy the chart and paste it into the other open document (unsaved).

16.   Leave the documents open for the next exercise.

Driving Lesson 96 - Cut and Paste Objects

P **Park and Read**

Objects such as images and charts can be removed from their original location and pasted to a different location within a document or in a different document. <u>When an object is cut the original is removed</u>.

Manoeuvres

1. Using the same documents as in the previous Driving Lesson, select a **cat** image from the unsaved document.

2. Click **Cut**, 📇, or use the key press <**Ctrl X**> to remove the image.

3. Click **Paste**, 📋, or use the key press <**Ctrl V**> to paste the cat back into the document.

4. Select the cat and cut it again.

5. Switch to **Objects**.

6. Paste the cat into this document.

7. Move to the other, unsaved document.

8. Cut the car and then paste it back into the same document.

9. Cut the chart and paste it back into the same document.

10. Cut the remaining objects from this document and paste them into **Objects**.

11. Save **Objects** and close it.

12. Close the other document, <u>without</u> saving.

Driving Lesson 97 - Revision

This covers the features introduced in this section. Try not to refer to the preceding Driving Lessons while completing it.

1. Start a new document.

2. Insert a **Clip Art** picture of your choice from any **Collection**.

3. Delete the picture.

4. Insert a different image from **Clip Art**.

5. Move the picture to the centre of the page.

6. Resize the picture to make it larger.

7. Add your name to the header.

8. Print one copy of the document.

9. Close the document <u>without</u> saving.

10. Open the document **Cat**.

11. Position the cursor at the end of the first paragraph and start a new line.

12. Insert the picture **cat** from the data files.

13. Resize the picture to about half its original size.

14. **Print Preview** the document.

15. Add your name and the date to the footer.

16. Print one copy of the document.

17. Close it <u>without</u> saving.

 Check the answers at the back of the guide for an indication of how your document should look.

If you experienced any difficulty completing the Revision, refer back to the Driving Lessons in this section. Then redo the Revision.

Once you are confident with the features, complete the Record of Achievement Matrix referring to the section at the end of the guide.

Answers

Driving Lesson 8

Step 9   a)   **New Blank Document**

         b)   **Paste**

         c)   **Print** (+ name of printer)

         d)   **Spelling and Grammar**

         e)   **Format Painter**

         f)   **Underline**

         g)   **Save**

         h)   **Numbering**

Step 11   There are 7 possible entries for **About getting help while you work**.

Driving Lesson 28

Step 5   The invisible area to the left of the document is called the **Selection Bar**.

Driving Lesson 32

Step 1   When the **Print** button is clicked one copy of the entire document is printed.

Step 2   The normal setting for the **Page Range** is **All**.

Step 3   The normal setting for the **Number of copies** is **1**.

Step 4   **Print Preview** shows the layout of the document and page breaks.

Step 12   The document contains **3** pages.

Driving Lesson 33

Step 14   Enter **1,3** in the **Pages** box of the **Page range** area.

Driving Lesson 42

Step 1   a)   **B** switches **Bold** formatting on or off

         b)   **I** switches **Italic** formatting on or off

         c)   **U** switches **Underline** formatting on or off

Step 2   A **Font** is a type or style of print. The menu command **Format | Font** displays the **Font** dialog box

Step 3   The colour of selected text can be changed either by using the **Font Color** button on the **Formatting** toolbar or via the **Font** dialog box.

Driving Lesson 52

Step 1   **11** possible spelling mistakes are highlighted in the document.

Step 8   **Find Next** can be clicked a further 4 times before the search finishes.

Step 14 There are **10** possible spelling mistakes indicated within the document.

Driving Lesson 78

AUTHOR	TITLE	TYPE
Jane Austen	Pride and Prejudice	Prose
William Shakespeare	Macbeth	Drama
William Shakespeare	Othello	Drama
Thomas Hardy	Jude the Obscure	Prose
Christina Rossetti	Goblin Market	Poetry
William Blake	The Tyger	Poetry
Christopher Marlowe	Doctor Faustus	Drama
Charles Dickens	Great Expectations	Prose
Charlotte Brontë	Jane Eyre	Prose
George Eliot	The Mill on the Floss	Prose

Driving Lesson 83

Step 4   The number of pages is reduced to 4.

Driving Lesson 97

Glossary

Alignment	Where text appears on the page in relation to the margins.
Application	A software program such as *Word*.
Commands	Selections from the **Menu Bar** which perform actions.
Copy & Paste	Duplicate text or images, etc. from one place to another within a document or between documents.
Cut & Paste	Remove text or images, etc. from one place and place them in another.
First Line Indent	Move the first line further in from the left margin than the others in a paragraph.
Font	A type or style of print.
Format	Change the way a document looks.
Headers & Footers	Common identification lines at the top and/or bottom of each page.
HTML	The format of web pages.
Justified	Straight left and right margins.
Orientation	The way up a page is - **Portrait** or **Landscape**.
Mail Merge	Combining a main document with a data source.
Print Preview	A feature that shows how a document will look before it is printed.
Save	Keep a copy of your file on the hard or floppy disk.
Selection Bar	A blank area at the left of the page, used to select text.
Styles	Pre-created formats consisting of paragraph and font formats.
Symbols	Special characters that are not on the keyboard.
Tabs	A precise measurement for aligning vertical rows of text.
Template	A base document that contains certain elements and can be used over and over again.
Undo & Redo	Features that allow you to reverse or reapply your last actions.
Web Page	Storage facility of internet information.
Word Wrap	How the computer automatically detects the end of a line and starts a new one.
Zoom	A feature that either allows the document to be viewed more closely, or more of the document, but in less detail.

Index

Record of Achievement Matrix

This Matrix is to be used to measure your progress while working through the guide. This is a learning reinforcement process, you judge when you are competent.

Tick boxes are provided for each feature. 1 is for no knowledge, 2 some knowledge and 3 is for competent. A section is only complete when column 3 is completed for all parts of the section.

For details on sitting ECDL Examinations in your country please contact the local ECDL Licensee or visit the European Computer Driving Licence Foundation Limited web site at http://www.ecdl.org.

Tick the Relevant Boxes **1**: No Knowledge   **2**: Some Knowledge   **3**: Competent

Section	No.	Driving Lesson	1	2	3
1 Getting Started	1	Starting Word			
	2	Layout of the Word Screen			
	3	Menu Bar			
	4	Toolbars			
	5	Task Pane			
	6	Help			
	7	The Office Assistant			
2 Documents	9	Entering Text			
	10	Saving Documents			
	11	Closing a Document/Word			
	12	Creating a New Document			
	13	Open an Existing Document			
	14	Views			
	15	Saving in a Different Format			
	16	Saving as a Template			
	17	Saving in Earlier Versions			
3 Editing Text	20	Inserting and Deleting Text			
	21	Select Words and Sentences			
	22	Select Lines and Paragraphs			
	23	Symbols			
	24	Undo and Redo			
	25	Show/Hide Characters			
	26	Soft Carriage Returns			
4 Printing	30	Previewing a Document			
	31	Printing a Document			
5 Formatting Text	34	Underline, Bold and Italic			
	35	Formatting of Selected Text			
	36	Fonts and Text Size			
	37	Changing Text Appearance			
	38	Subscript and Superscript			
	39	Changing Case			
	40	Format Painter			
	41	Cut, Copy and Paste			
6 Tools	45	Spelling Checker			
	46	Add to Dictionary			
	47	Hyphenation			
	48	Searching a Document			
	49	Replace			
	50	Zoom Control			
	51	Preferences			

Tick the Relevant Boxes **1**: No Knowledge   **2**: Some Knowledge   **3**: Competent

Section	No.	Driving Lesson	1	2	3
7 Formatting Paragraphs	54	Alignment			
	55	Indenting Paragraphs			
	56	Advanced Indentation			
	57	Numbering			
	58	Bullets			
	59	Line Spacing			
	60	Spacing Between Paragraphs			
	61	Tab Settings			
	62	Tab Alignment			
	63	Adding Borders			
8 Multiple Documents	66	Switch Between Documents			
	67	Cut, Copy, Paste Between Documents			
	68	Headers and Footers			
	69	Page Numbering			
9 Tables	72	Tables			
	73	Entering Text			
	74	Selecting Cells			
	75	Changing Column Width/Row Height			
	76	Inserting and Deleting Rows/Columns			
	77	Table Borders/Shading			
10 Document Manipulation	80	Document Setup			
	81	Page Breaks			
	82	Styles			
11 Mail Merge	84	Mail Merge			
	85	Creating the Main Document			
	86	Creating a Data Source			
	87	Editing the Main Document			
	88	Merging			
	89	Open a data Source			
12 Objects	92	Inserting a Picture			
	93	Inserting Charts			
	94	Move and Resize Objects			
	95	Copy and Paste Objects			
	96	Cut and Paste Objects			

Other Products from CiA Training Ltd

CiA Training Ltd is a leading publishing company, which has consistently delivered the highest quality products since 1985. A wide range of flexible and easy to use self teach resources has been developed by CiA's experienced publishing team to aid the learning process. These include the following ECDL Foundation approved products at the time of publication of this product:

- **ECDL/ICDL Syllabus 5.0**

- **ECDL/ICDL Advanced Syllabus 2.0**

- **ECDL/ICDL Revision Series**

- **ECDL/ICDL Advanced Syllabus 2.0 Revision Series**

- **e-Citizen**

Previous syllabus versions also available - contact us for further details.

We hope you have enjoyed using our materials and would love to hear your opinions about them. If you'd like to give us some feedback, please go to:

www.ciatraining.co.uk/feedback.php

and let us know what you think.

New products are constantly being developed. For up to the minute information on our products, to view our full range, to find out more, or to be added to our mailing list, visit:

www.ciatraining.co.uk